ADVENTURES IN LEADERSHIP

A Practical Guide to Exceptional Leadership

Get ready to step into the leadership limelight! This super-friendly handbook slices leadership wisdom into five juicy pieces, tailor-made for those stepping up, dipping their toes, or taking their first steps as leaders. Bursting with real-world stories and hands-on exercises, this guide will have you rocking your leadership journey and creating ripples of positivity in your team and beyond.

Personal Note

Have you noticed tv commercials many times will repeat? The reason for that is repetition promotes memory. Hearing or seeing something multiple times helps to embed the information in our long-term memory. Additionally, repetition can help us better recall information when we need it. You will see repetition multiple times throughout this book and that is by design.

Introduction

Let's Dive into Leadership Magic!

Welcome to a world of exciting possibilities, where you're about to uncover the wonderful world of leadership awesomeness. We're excited to have you on this journey as we unlock the power of five fantastic leadership principles that are going to turbocharge your leadership game.

Think of this book as your trusty sidekick, your guide to becoming the leader you've always admired. Whether you're a fresh face stepping onto the leadership stage, a starry-eyed newbie eager to make a mark, or just someone looking to take their leadership skills up a notch, we've got your back.

Leadership isn't about fancy titles or secret handshakes. Nope, it's all about connecting, inspiring, and making things happen. And guess what? You're totally capable of doing just that. It's not rocket science; it's more like leadership magic that you can wield to create a positive impact on your team, your workplace, and even the whole wide world.

So, buckle up and get ready to embark on a journey filled with high-fives, aha moments, and plenty of smiles. We're here to make learning about leadership as fun as a rollercoaster ride and as satisfying as your favorite comfort food. Are you ready to dive in and uncover the secrets of being an awesome leader? Let's do this!

Sneak Peek: The 5 Fantastic Leadership Principles

You're in for a treat because we're about to spill the beans on the five game-changing leadership principles that will have you strutting your stuff like a leadership champion. These principles are like the supercharger that turns good leaders into downright legends.

1. **Rockstar Communication:** Get ready to charm your way into hearts with your silver-tongued prowess. We'll show you how to listen like a pro, speak like a poet, and give feedback that leaves everyone cheering for an encore.

2. **Team Harmony and You:** Discover the magic of building a harmonious crew, setting goals that make their eyes light up, and finding out your teammates' superpowers (spoiler: they all have 'em!).

3. **Unleash Your Inner Captain:** Captain Delegation to the rescue! Learn how to trust your team to take the helm, make decisions like a champ, and grow their skills faster than a sunflower in summer.

4. **Problem-Busting and Change High-fives:** Say hello to your superhero cape as you tackle challenges head-on, solve problems like a puzzle pro, and dance through change like it's a party.

5. **Team Spirit Spark:** Time to sprinkle some stardust! Celebrate successes like a rockstar, connect your team's work to a bigger purpose, and shower them with appreciation like confetti.

These principles are your roadmap to leadership awesomeness, and we're here to guide you through each one with high-fives, relatable stories, and more 'aha' moments than you ever thought possible. Get ready to unlock your potential and dazzle the world with your leadership prowess!

Chapter 1

Rockstar Communication

Get ready to unleash your inner chatterbox as we dive headfirst into the world of communication. This chapter is like your very own treasure map, guiding you through the lands of active listening, message crafting, and the art of feedback.

Having a real conversation is like a dance of words where you both move together listening and speaking, the words flow between the two of you in perfect rhythm. That's the power of active listening. We'll teach you the ninja moves to listen with your ears, your eyes, and even your heart – because great leaders know that listening isn't just about hearing words; it's about understanding feelings and vibes too.

But hold up, it's not all ears and no talk! Your words are like little bursts of communication that can make things happen. We'll show you how to weave messages that are as clear as a mountain spring and as engaging as a Netflix binge. Have you ever heard of the "feedback charm"? It's not as mystical as it sounds, but it can work wonders in boosting your team's growth.

So, if you're ready to level up your communication game and become the rockstar conversationalist you were always meant to be, let's dive into the captivating world of rockstar communication!

Unlocking the Art of Amazing Conversations

Think of this chapter as your ticket to a world where every word is a brushstroke on the canvas of connection, where dialogues become dances and stories are spun with the threads of understanding.

In the realm of leadership, every conversation is a chance to step into that spotlight and shine. Unlocking the art of amazing conversations isn't just about words; it's about creating a harmonious symphony of connection, understanding, and engagement. As you embark on this journey, let's delve into the intricacies of crafting conversations that resonate and leave a lasting impact.

Embrace the Dance of Deep Listening: The Symphony of Leadership Connection

In the realm of leadership, deep listening is akin to being immersed in this concert experience. It's more than just hearing words; it's about attuning your senses to the subtle cues, the raw emotions, and the unspoken messages conveyed by the speaker.

Unlocking the art of deep listening requires more than passive attention. Let's explore the "Three Rs" – Receive, Reflect, and Respond – as the notes that compose your creation of effective communication.

Receive: Tune into the Speaker

Imagine you're an avid fan, leaning forward to catch every note from the stage. When engaged in conversation, receiving the speaker's words should be no less captivating. Here's how to receive effectively:

The Gift of Presence: Convey your full presence in the moment. Maintain unwavering eye contact, signaling that you're fully invested in the conversation. This non-verbal gesture assures the speaker that they have your complete attention.

Non-verbal Harmonies: Employ affirmative non-verbal cues – nods of understanding, smiles of encouragement, or expressions mirroring empathy. These cues resonate like harmonious chords in the conversation, reassuring the speaker that their message is valued.

Strategic Notetaking: In certain situations, take notes to aid your listening. This is particularly useful during complex discussions or when action items need to be remembered. Jot down key points or insights, ensuring they're not lost in the midst of conversation.

Reflect: Harmonize with the Speaker

Imagine the lingering notes after a powerful performance. In conversations, reflection is akin to savoring those notes, processing their meaning, and conveying your understanding. Here's how to reflect effectively:

Paraphrase the Message: Summarize the speaker's key points in your own words. This not only demonstrates your active engagement but also ensures you've grasped the essence of their message. For instance, if a team member discusses project challenges, you might say, "It sounds like managing the project timeline is posing some challenges."

Seek Clarification: If any aspect of the conversation is unclear, don't hesitate to seek clarification. Encourage the speaker to expand on their thoughts by asking questions like, "Could you provide more context on that?" or "Can you share an example?"

Respond: Craft Your Conversation Input

Responding is your moment to add your notes to the conversation masterpiece, to offer your own melody in response to what you've heard. Here's how to respond effectively:

Empathetic Response: Respond with empathy, acknowledging the speaker's emotions and perspectives. If a team member shares concerns about a project, respond with understanding: "I can see how managing the project timeline might be challenging. Let's explore solutions together."

Constructive Response: If the situation calls for it, provide constructive feedback. Share your insights and suggestions in a supportive manner, emphasizing collaboration and joint problem-solving.

Encourage (Always): Your team respects and will respond to your words. Always let them know that you believe in them. Encourage them to think outside the box and personalize the task at hand.

Here are just a few instances where listening intently is especially critical:

Team Brainstorming: During brainstorming sessions, receive each idea with open curiosity, reflect on their potential, and respond with appreciation and constructive input.

Conflict Resolution: In conflict resolution, receive each party's perspective, reflect on their concerns, and respond by facilitating a dialogue that seeks common ground.

Coaching Conversations: During coaching conversations, receive your team member's career aspirations, reflect on their development needs, and respond with a personalized growth plan.

Deep listening transforms conversations into harmonious exchanges. By embracing the "Three Rs" – Receive, Reflect and Respond – you create an atmosphere where your team members feel valued, heard, and truly understood, ultimately fostering trust, collaboration, and shared success.

Curiosity: Your Passport to Authentic Connection

Imagine yourself in a vibrant and diverse music festival, wandering from one stage to another, exploring the various genres and styles of music. Just as you navigate through the festival grounds, curiosity can be your passport to authentic and meaningful connections in your conversations. It's a powerful tool that allows you to delve into the landscapes of your team members' thoughts and emotions, fostering a deeper understanding of their perspectives and experiences. To unlock this aspect of curiosity, embrace your inner explorer and learn the art of asking open-ended questions that invite richer insights and facilitate more profound conversations.

Curiosity goes beyond surface-level inquiries; it's about genuinely seeking to understand others. When you engage in a conversation with a curious mindset, you display a sincere interest in what the other person has to say. This act alone can significantly enhance the quality of your interactions and build stronger connections with your team.

Consider incorporating open-ended questions into your conversations. These are queries that cannot be answered with a simple "yes" or "no" but require more extended and thoughtful responses. Questions like, "Could you share more about your approach to solving the problem?" or "What led you to consider this particular solution?" invite the speaker to provide in-depth explanations and insights. Such questions not only demonstrate your interest but also encourage the speaker to delve into their thought process, leading to richer and more meaningful conversations.

By asking open-ended questions, you create a safe and inviting space for your team members to express themselves. They feel heard, valued, and understood, fostering a sense of trust and openness. This openness can lead to more transparent and authentic conversations, allowing you to get to know your team members on a deeper level.

Curiosity also plays a significant role in building empathy, which is a cornerstone of authentic connection. When you actively seek to understand the thoughts, feelings, and experiences of your team members, you demonstrate empathy. This, in turn, makes your team members feel acknowledged and validated. Empathetic leadership creates a supportive and inclusive environment where team members are more likely to open up and share their concerns, ideas, and aspirations.

Moreover, curiosity contributes to the development of a growth mindset. It encourages you to view each conversation as an opportunity to learn and grow, both personally and professionally. When you approach interactions with curiosity, you're open to different perspectives and experiences. This openness fosters a culture of continuous learning and improvement within your team.

The art of curiosity can be particularly beneficial during challenging conversations or when addressing conflicts. Instead of making assumptions or judgments, approach these situations with a genuine desire to understand. By asking questions like, "What has led to these concerns?" or "Can you share your perspective on this issue?" you create an environment where team members feel safe to express their feelings and concerns. This not only helps in resolving conflicts more effectively but also strengthens relationships within the team.

Curiosity also enhances problem-solving and decision-making processes. When you're curious, you explore different angles and possibilities, which can lead to more creative and innovative solutions. It encourages critical thinking and a comprehensive examination of issues, ultimately leading to better outcomes.

Curiosity promotes a culture of inclusion and diversity. By actively seeking to understand the diverse perspectives within your team, you create an environment where everyone's voice is valued. This not only fosters a sense of belonging but also brings a broader range of ideas and experiences to the table, enhancing the team's problem-solving capabilities and innovation.

To harness the power of curiosity in your leadership, practice active listening. When engaged in a conversation, focus on the speaker, maintain eye contact, and avoid interrupting. Let them finish their thoughts before responding. This demonstrates your respect and genuine interest in their perspective.

Moreover, make curiosity a habit. Consistently ask open-ended questions during your interactions and challenge yourself to explore new areas and viewpoints. Encourage your team to do the same, creating a culture where curiosity is not only appreciated but expected.

Curiosity is your passport to authentic connection with your team members. It allows you to explore the diverse landscapes of their thoughts and emotions, creating a deeper understanding and stronger connections. By asking open-ended questions, you demonstrate your interest and invite richer insights, fostering more meaningful conversations. Curiosity promotes empathy, trust, and transparency within the team, leading to a culture of inclusion, diversity, and continuous learning. As a leader, embrace curiosity as a valuable tool to unlock the full potential of your team and build authentic connections that drive success.

Understanding the Power of Presence and Patience

Leadership is an intricate art, and at its core, it revolves around effective communication. Amidst the myriad skills that leaders must master, one aspect stands out as indispensable - the ability to listen. In the world of leadership, the power of presence and patience cannot be overstated. In this discourse, we will delve into the nuances of these essential qualities and how they significantly impact leadership effectiveness.

Leaders who wield influence with grace understand the importance of being truly present in the moment. This isn't just a matter of being physically there; it's about engaging your mind and emotions in the conversation. The power of presence means giving your undivided attention to the speaker, tuning in to both their words and the underlying emotions.

Presence requires setting aside distractions. The modern world is replete with interruptions, from constant notifications on our devices to the myriad responsibilities vying for our attention. To truly listen, a leader must consciously put aside these distractions, creating a sacred space for the conversation.

A critical aspect of presence is resisting the urge to formulate your response while the speaker is still talking. Often, in our eagerness to contribute, we begin crafting our replies before the speaker has even completed their thoughts. True presence necessitates withholding this impulse, allowing the speaker to express themselves fully before you start crafting your response.

The Essence of Patience in Leadership

Equally important to presence is patience. Patience in leadership entails allowing the conversation to unfold organically. This means not rushing the speaker or pushing the conversation in a particular direction prematurely. Instead, it involves letting the discussion progress naturally, giving every participant the time they need to express themselves fully.

Patience also means taking a moment before responding. This brief pause is not a sign of hesitation but a mark of respect for the speaker. It gives their words a chance to settle and resonate, ensuring they feel heard and valued.

Consider a scenario where a team member presents an innovative idea. An impatient response might be, "I'll get back to you with my thoughts on that." However, a patient response acknowledges the idea, recognizes its value, and conveys a willingness to engage further. It might sound like, "I hadn't thought of that before. I'll need some time to fully digest it, but let's reconvene to explore how we can potentially make it a reality." This kind of response shows the speaker that their input is not only appreciated but also taken seriously.

The Psychological Impact of Listening

To understand the deep-seated importance of presence and patience, we must recognize the profound psychological impact of listening. When we truly listen to someone, we validate their experiences and emotions. This validation creates a sense of trust and respect, which are the cornerstones of any healthy relationship, including the leader-follower relationship.

Active listening fosters empathy. As a leader, empathy is a crucial trait. It allows you to step into the shoes of your team members, understanding their perspectives and concerns. When you exhibit empathy through your patient and present listening, it fosters a culture of compassion and understanding within the team.

Listening also has the power to resolve conflicts. In any group dynamic, disagreements and conflicts are bound to arise. However, when leaders listen attentively and patiently, they can often defuse tense situations by allowing everyone to express their viewpoints. This, in turn, paves the way for collaborative problem-solving and conflict resolution.

The Impact on Decision-Making

Listening isn't merely a passive act; it's an active part of decision-making. When leaders take the time to listen carefully to their team members, they gain valuable insights and perspectives. This, in turn, enriches the quality of decisions made.

Consider a leader faced with a pivotal decision. They have the option to either rely solely on their own judgment or to listen to their team's input. The former may yield a decision rooted in one perspective, while the latter brings diverse viewpoints to the table. By being present and patient in their interactions, the leader can gather crucial information, ensuring that their decisions are more well-rounded and informed.

When leaders involve their team in the decision-making process through active listening, they create a sense of ownership and buy-in among team members. Team members who feel heard and valued are more likely to be invested in the outcomes of the decisions, leading to increased commitment and motivation.

The Role of Feedback

Feedback is a fundamental component of effective leadership, and it is intricately tied to presence and patience. When leaders are present in their interactions, they create a safe space for open and honest feedback. Team members are more likely to express their thoughts and concerns when they feel that their leader is truly listening.

Patience in the context of feedback means allowing team members to share their thoughts without interruption. This ensures that they can express themselves fully and that their feedback is understood in its entirety.

In the same vein, leaders who exhibit patience in receiving feedback are more likely to encourage a culture of continuous improvement. When team members see that their input is taken seriously and not met with immediate resistance or defensiveness, they are more inclined to offer feedback regularly. This, in turn, leads to a more agile and responsive team and organization.

Building Trust and Credibility

Trust is the bedrock of effective leadership. Trust is not something that can be demanded; it must be earned. Listening, with presence and patience, is one of the most powerful ways to build trust within a team.

When leaders consistently practice active listening, they demonstrate that they value their team members' thoughts and opinions. This, in turn, fosters trust as team members feel that their leader has their best interests at heart. Trust leads to credibility, which is the cornerstone of leadership influence.

Credibility is vital because it is the linchpin of influence. Leaders who are credible find it easier to rally their team around a shared vision, persuade stakeholders, and navigate through challenges. The ability to influence is often what sets effective leaders apart from others.

Overcoming Communication Barriers

Communication barriers are a common challenge in any organization. These barriers can stem from differences in culture, language, or even just personal communication styles. When leaders practice presence and patience in their interactions, they are better equipped to overcome these barriers.

In a multicultural or diverse team, for example, presence means respecting and embracing different communication styles. Patience entails giving team members from diverse backgrounds the time they need to express themselves, even if their language proficiency is not as strong as others. By doing so, leaders create an inclusive environment where all voices are valued, regardless of the language or cultural differences.

In situations where team members have varying communication styles, some may be more reserved, while others may be more assertive. Being present and patient allows leaders to adapt to these different styles, ensuring that everyone has the opportunity to contribute.

The Impact on Innovation

Innovation is a driving force in today's business world, and it often stems from the ability to think creatively and share new ideas. Leaders who excel at presence and patience create an environment that is conducive to innovation.

Innovative ideas often require a nurturing environment where team members feel comfortable sharing their thoughts and ideas, no matter how unconventional they may seem. Being present and patient in your interactions fosters such an environment. It shows that you are open to new ideas and that you value the creativity of your team.

Mirroring: A Gesture of Empathy

In conversations, mirroring is your gesture of empathy, reflecting back the speaker's emotions to establish a deeper connection. This can be done through nonverbal cues such as nodding, mirroring body language, and expressing empathy through facial expressions.

For instance, if a team member expresses frustration about a project setback, you might mirror their emotion by nodding sympathetically and saying, "I understand that this setback has been challenging for you." This simple act validates their feelings and fosters a sense of understanding.

Storytelling: Creating Bridges of Connection

Using stories can be the most effective tool you can use. Many times, it can convey ideas and precepts that can be difficult for your team to comprehend any other way. Imagine a campfire, where stories create an atmosphere of camaraderie and connection. In conversations, storytelling is your tool to create bridges between your experiences and the speaker's. Unlock this art by sharing relevant anecdotes that illustrate shared challenges, triumphs, or lessons learned.

Suppose a team member is grappling with a difficult decision. You might share a personal story about a similar crossroads you faced in your career, recounting how you navigated the situation and the outcomes it yielded. This not only offers guidance but also humanizes your leadership and fosters a sense of relationship.

Unlocking the art of amazing conversations is a journey that encompasses deep listening, curiosity, presence, empathy, and storytelling. As you practice these elements, picture yourself as a conductor directing a series of profound and meaningful conversations. Each interaction becomes an opportunity to foster understanding, inspire collaboration, and forge authentic connections.

Every conversation is a canvas on which you paint your leadership legacy. Just as a musician crafts melodies that touch the heart, your conversations have the power to resonate and leave a lasting impact on your team.

So, my conversation virtuoso, embrace the art of amazing conversations with intention and enthusiasm. Step into the spotlight, engage with empathy, and let your words create a harmony of connection that echoes through your leadership journey.

Give a Listen, Earn Respect

Picture yourself in a room, enveloped in a conversation where the spoken words aren't merely sounds, but gateways to a world of thoughts, emotions, and ideas. In this moment, you're not a passive observer; you are an active participant, delving into the symphony of someone's mind and heart. It's akin to unearthing a treasure map, one that leads you to the innermost core of their being. When you bestow the gift of your undivided attention, it's not just a polite gesture – it's a profound demonstration of respect. It's a declaration that screams, "You matter, and what you have to say holds immense value."

Listening is not just a mundane act; it's an art form, a craft that transcends the mere act of sound waves striking your eardrums. It's about being wholly present, fully engaged with the speaker on a level that goes far beyond the auditory realm. In the realm of conversations, being an exceptional listener equates to being a cherished confidant. A confidant who doesn't merely nod in agreement but plunges headlong into the ocean of words, relentlessly searching for those pearls of wisdom and profound understanding.

And let's not underestimate the enchanting transformation that unfolds when you lend your ears. The respect you garner in return is akin to acquiring a precious gem to adorn your treasury of relationships. People feel cherished and validated when they realize their words are not merely evaporating into the ether; there's someone on the other end who genuinely cares about their thoughts and feelings.

So, get ready to harness the incredible power of listening. As you embark on this journey, keep in mind that respect extends beyond mere courtesy; it's about crafting connections, nurturing relationships, and weaving a tapestry of understanding that spans the vast expanse of human interaction.

Messages that Sparkle: Simple and Clear

If conversations were a blockbuster movie, your words would be the stars of the show. They have the power to dazzle, inspire, and evoke emotions that linger long after the final credits roll. But here's the catch: for your words to shine brightly, they need to be crafted with care and precision.

Have you ever encountered a message that left you scratching your head, wondering what exactly the sender meant? We've all been there, and it's not the most pleasant experience. In a world buzzing with information and messages, simplicity is your best friend. It's the guiding star that ensures your words reach their intended destination without getting lost in translation.

Crafting messages that sparkle with simplicity and clarity is akin to becoming a wordsmith armed with a transformative pen. You have the power to turn complex ideas and intricate concepts into easily digestible nuggets of wisdom. You transform convoluted jargon into straightforward sentences that pack a punch. You take the puzzle pieces of communication and assemble them in a way that leaves no room for ambiguity.

Imagine sending an email that instantly gets the point across, without the need for multiple rounds of back-and-forth. Envision leading a team meeting where everyone leaves with a crystal-clear understanding of the objectives. It's not a pipe dream; it's the result of mastering the art of crafting messages that sparkle.

But here's the kicker: simplicity doesn't mean dullness. It's about finding the perfect balance between clarity and engagement. Your words should dance off the page or screen, captivating the reader's attention while effortlessly delivering the intended message.

Let's envision the practicality of this art. Consider a complex email communication where intricate details often lead to confusion. Here's how to transform it into a simple and comprehensible exchange:

Example 1: From Complexity to Clarity - Project Update Email

Complex Version:

Subject: Monthly Project Status Report

Dear Team,

I hope this message finds you well. As part of our ongoing commitment to transparency and comprehensive project management, I'm pleased to provide you with the latest update on our monthly project status. Please find attached a detailed report, including progress metrics, financial analysis, and a breakdown of resource allocation.

Should you have any questions or require further clarification, don't hesitate to reach out to me. We will also be scheduling a follow-up meeting to discuss the specifics in more detail.

Thank you for your continued dedication to this project.

Simple and Clear Version:

Subject: Quick Project Update

Hi Team,

I wanted to drop a quick note to update you on our project's status. Things are progressing well, and we're on track. If you have any

questions or need more details, feel free to reach out. We'll schedule a meeting next week to dive deeper.

Thanks for your hard work!

In this simplified version, the message retains its essence while shedding unnecessary complexity, making it easier for the recipients to grasp the core information.

Example 2: From Complexity to Clarity - Team Meeting Agenda

Complex Version:

Subject: Agenda for the Upcoming Team Meeting

Dear Team,

I hope this message finds you in good health. As our next team meeting approaches, I'm sharing the agenda to help you prepare. We will discuss various topics, including project updates, departmental goals, and upcoming deadlines. Additionally, we'll touch upon individual performance metrics and explore potential process improvements.

Your active participation is encouraged, and I welcome your insights and suggestions. Please come prepared to engage in a constructive dialogue that contributes to our team's success.

Thank you for your dedication and commitment to our collective goals.

Simple and Clear Version:

Subject: Team Meeting Agenda

Hi Team,

Our next meeting is coming up. We'll cover project updates, department goals, and upcoming deadlines. We'll also talk about performance and process improvements. Your input is important, so come ready to share ideas.

Thanks for your dedication!

By simplifying the message and focusing on key points, the agenda becomes more accessible and engaging for the recipients.

Example 3: From Complexity to Clarity - Client Proposal

Complex Version:

Subject: Proposal - Comprehensive Marketing Strategy

Dear Team,

I'm excited to share our proposal. It outlines a comprehensive marketing strategy that incorporates multi-channel marketing, customer segmentation, and data-driven analytics. We've considered their unique needs and market trends to develop a personalized approach that maximizes ROI.

In the attached document, you'll find detailed insights into our strategy, including campaign timelines, budget allocation, and KPIs. We believe this proposal aligns perfectly with the objectives and positions us as a strategic partner for their marketing success.

Please review the proposal, and we'll schedule a meeting to discuss any questions or modifications.

Simple and Clear Version:

Subject: Marketing Proposal

Hi Team,

Here's our proposal for the marketing strategy. It covers all the details, like when we'll run campaigns, where the budget goes, and how we'll measure success. Check it out, and let's talk after you've had a chance to read it.

Thanks for your hard work!

In this version, the message retains its essence but becomes more accessible and reader-friendly.

Example 4: From Complexity to Clarity - Project Kick-off Message

Complex Version:

Subject: Project Kick-off Meeting Announcement

Dear Team,

I trust this message finds you in good health and high spirits. As we embark on our exciting new project, I am pleased to announce the kick-off meeting scheduled for next Tuesday. During this meeting, we will delve into the project's objectives, scope, and deliverables. We will also introduce key stakeholders and discuss the roles and responsibilities within the project team.

Please come prepared with any questions or insights you may have. Your active participation will be instrumental in ensuring a successful project launch.

Looking forward to our journey together!

Simple and Clear Version:

Subject: Project Kick-off Meeting

Hi Team,

Our project kick-off meeting is next Tuesday. We'll talk about what we're doing, who's involved, and what we need to do. If you have any questions, bring them. Your input matters!

Let's get started!

In this simplified version, the message communicates the essential details in a clear and straightforward manner.

These examples illustrate how simplifying communication can enhance comprehension and engagement. By focusing on clarity, you ensure your messages are easily understood and leave no room for misinterpretation, making your leadership communication more effective.

So, dear wordsmith, get ready to dip your pen in the ink of clarity and sprinkle your messages with the stardust of simplicity. As you journey through this enchanting landscape, remember that your words have the power to illuminate minds and hearts, to bridge gaps, and to create connections that withstand the test of time.

High Fives and Helpful Hints: Nailing Feedback

Get ready to celebrate a feedback fiesta, where positivity reigns supreme and every nugget of advice carries the promise of growth and every critique is a stepping stone towards becoming an even better version of yourself. Constructive feedback is where transformation thrives and hope becomes an anchor.

Feedback, often misunderstood, is the unsung hero of personal and professional development. It's not the dreaded monster under the bed; it's the superhero cape that empowers you to soar to new heights. Think of feedback as your loyal companion on the journey to improvement, a compass guiding you toward mastery and a mirror reflecting both your strengths and untapped potential.

Now, you might be pondering, "How can I offer feedback that doesn't deflate spirits but instead nurtures growth?" Fear not, intrepid explorer, for we possess the treasure map to navigate these uncharted waters. The secret lies in cloaking your feedback with a blanket of encouragement and serving it with a side of instruction.

Imagine yourself as the coach of a championship-winning sports team. Your feedback is akin to a playbook, guiding your players towards victory. Just as you emphasize their standout performances, you gently highlight areas that could use some fine-tuning. Your role, much like a coach, isn't to tear down but to uplift, empower, and cultivate an environment of continuous enhancement.

However, here's the delightful twist: feedback isn't a monologue; it's a dialogue. It's a conversation that hinges on active listening, empathy, and the willingness to evolve. When you extend an invitation to receive feedback, you're not merely displaying humility; you're signifying your commitment to growth and demonstrating your respect for the perspectives of those around you.

Elevating Others Through Affirmation

Positive feedback is akin to a magnifying glass, focusing on the brilliant aspects of someone's performance and illuminating their path to success. Imagine each member of your team as a shining star, and your positive feedback as the constellation that guides them through their professional journey.

When offering positive feedback, go beyond acknowledging the task accomplished; delve into the qualities that made it exceptional. Let each team member know that you believe in them, that they are not just capable but brimming with untapped potential. For instance, rather than saying, "Good job on the presentation," you might say, "Your presentation was captivating. Your clear articulation and creative visuals truly showcased our exceptional communication skills. I have no doubt you'll continue to excel in this area."

Empathy: The Heart of Constructive Critique

Now, let's venture into the realm of constructive feedback. Think of it as a sculptor's chisel, meticulously shaping a masterpiece. Constructive feedback is an opportunity to collaboratively refine skills and cultivate growth. Picture yourself as a mentor, guiding your team members along a path of improvement.

Start with empathy. Imagine walking in the other person's shoes, understanding their challenges and aspirations. This foundation of empathy shapes how you deliver your feedback. Approach the conversation with the intention to empower, not discourage. Instead of saying, "You made a mistake in the report," you might say, "I noticed a small error in the report, but I'm confident you have the skills to correct it. Let's work together to ensure the final version shines."

Creating an Environment of Growth

In the vast landscape of human interaction and personal development, feedback is the delicate conductor of change, orchestrating the symphony of growth. Every interaction, every conversation, and every word of feedback has the potential to uplift individuals and elevate them to new heights. It is a transformative tool that can reshape perspectives, ignite passions, and pave the path to excellence.

Positive feedback, often regarded as the cornerstone of personal and professional development, serves as a powerful affirmation that nurtures confidence and fuels one's potential. When it's delivered genuinely and thoughtfully, it has the remarkable ability to inspire and motivate. It recognizes accomplishments and encourages the continuation of positive behaviors and actions. In essence, positive feedback is the sunlight that nourishes the seeds of greatness within individuals, allowing them to flourish and reach for the stars.

On the other hand, constructive feedback, when wielded with care and intention, becomes a catalyst for improvement. It is an invitation to embark on a journey of continuous enhancement. Constructive feedback, despite its often-critical nature, is the cornerstone of personal growth. It identifies areas for improvement, offering a roadmap for advancement. This type of feedback, when given effectively, acknowledges the existing potential for growth and provides a clear direction for how to achieve it.

As you step into the realm of feedback, envision yourself as a virtuoso, a maestro of influence and empowerment. Every word you speak, every insight you share, and every piece of feedback you provide carries the potential for transformation. Your role is not just to inform; it's to inspire and guide, helping individuals reach their full potential.

Your feedback isn't merely words; it's a source of strength, encouragement, and enlightenment. By offering positive feedback that affirms potential and constructive feedback that fosters growth, you're not just shaping the people around you; you're sculpting a culture of excellence and advancement. This culture, nurtured by your guidance, has the power to create a ripple effect, touching not only the individuals within your immediate sphere but also influencing the broader community in which you operate.

Now, as you journey forward in your feedback endeavors, consider the long-term impact of your words and insights. Feedback is not just a momentary exchange; it's an investment in someone's future. Each piece of feedback you provide, whether positive or constructive, has the potential to contribute to a lifetime of development and success.

Positive feedback, for example, can create a reservoir of confidence that individuals can draw upon during challenging times. When someone knows they are capable of excellence, they are more likely to push their boundaries and take on new challenges. Your words of encouragement become their inner voice, driving them to achieve even more.

Constructive feedback, when delivered effectively, serves as a road map for growth. It identifies specific areas that need improvement and provides actionable steps to achieve that improvement. As you continue to provide constructive feedback, you become a trusted source of guidance for those you mentor or lead. They will come to rely on your insights and knowledge, confident that your feedback will help them evolve and excel.

Let your feedback be the guiding star that leads your team to greatness. Your commitment to their growth is not just an act of leadership; it's a testament to your exceptional leadership. Your ability to inspire, motivate, and guide others through your feedback is the hallmark of a true leader. It fosters a sense of trust and loyalty within your team, as they recognize that you have their best interests at heart.

In building this culture of growth and excellence, it's essential to cultivate open communication. Encourage your team members to seek feedback from you and from each other. Create an environment where feedback is seen as a valuable resource for personal and collective development. In such an environment, individuals feel safe in sharing their thoughts and ideas, knowing that they will be met with respect and consideration.

As a feedback virtuoso, you should always be open to receiving feedback yourself. Just as you provide feedback to others, you should be receptive to the insights and perspectives of those around you. This not only sets a positive example but also allows you to continuously improve your own abilities as a leader and mentor.

As you navigate the intricate world of feedback, keep in mind that the symphony of growth is an ongoing, ever-evolving masterpiece. Every interaction, every conversation, and every piece of feedback contributes to this grand composition. With your guidance, individuals will flourish, teams will excel, and the culture of excellence you foster will endure as a lasting legacy. Your words and insights will reverberate through time, inspiring others to reach for their full potential and create their own symphonies of growth.

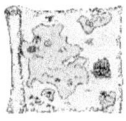

Chapter 2

Team Harmony and You

In this dynamic chapter, we're diving headfirst into the mesmerizing waters of team dynamics, where you'll master the art of building a harmonious crew that's ready to conquer challenges and celebrate victories together. So, grab your leadership compass, and let's embark on a thrilling expedition through the heart of teamwork and unity!

Crafting a Collaborative Crew

Envision your team as a dynamic ensemble, brimming with energy and innovation. You, in your role as the captain of leadership, stand at the helm, ready to create a masterpiece that harmonizes abilities, personalities, and expertise into a work of art. Here, collaboration transcends a mere catchphrase; it's the skill of melding diverse elements to craft an exquisite composition that satisfies the palette of success. Building a cohesive team isn't a matter of chance; it's a deliberate orchestration of minds and competencies.

In the journey of teamwork, the emphasis goes beyond mere coexistence; it revolves around fostering an environment where individual talents seamlessly converge to achieve collective excellence. The true art lies in adeptly managing and harmonizing a variety of personalities, skill sets, and perspectives to cultivate a high-performing and unified team.

Cohesion and Collaboration

Fostering cohesion and collaboration within a team is a multifaceted endeavor, and it begins with the establishment of a clear and compelling vision. Think of this vision as the unifying thread that binds each team member together, providing a shared purpose that motivates and guides everyone. In essence, the vision is the compass that points the way to collective success, serving as a source of inspiration and direction for the entire team.

This shared vision isn't just a mere statement of objectives; it's a call to action, a rallying cry that resonates with every team member. It should ignite passion and enthusiasm, encouraging individuals to wholeheartedly invest in the collective journey. When crafting a vision, it's essential to consider the bigger picture and the long-term goals. Think about what success looks like and what impact your team can make in the grand scheme of things.

Equally important is the effective communication of this vision. As a leader, you must champion this vision, becoming its most vocal advocate. Consistency in your messaging is crucial, as it reinforces the vision and keeps it at the forefront of everyone's minds. Your passion and commitment to the vision are contagious; they inspire others to buy into the shared goal and invest their efforts in achieving it.

One effective way to communicate the vision is through storytelling. Share stories of the journey ahead, emphasizing how each team member's role contributes to the collective success. Human beings are naturally drawn to stories, and they can relate to narratives that make the vision more tangible and relatable. It's not just about the destination; it's also about the adventure, the challenges, and the sense of purpose that the journey provides.

Open lines of communication are crucial in this phase. Encourage team members to share their thoughts, insights, and even their own vision of the future. This open dialogue not only strengthens the sense of ownership but also brings diverse perspectives to the table, enriching the vision with new insights.

As you navigate towards the shared vision, celebrate small successes along the way. Acknowledge and affirm individual and collective achievements to reinforce the team's belief in the shared vision. This practice not only demonstrates that progress is being made but also that the journey is worthwhile and achievable. Recognition and encouragement become the fuel that keeps the team's motivation burning.

In the realm of collaboration, there's no such thing as over-communication. Keep the vision alive and dynamic by reiterating it regularly and connecting it to day-to-day tasks and activities. This not only keeps everyone aligned but also provides a constant reminder of the overarching purpose, instilling a sense of direction and unity.

Creating a collaborative team isn't about randomly putting together a group of individuals. It's a deliberate blend of talents, skills, and personalities, all working in harmony toward a common goal. Each team member should not only understand the vision but also see how their unique strengths and attributes contribute to it. They should feel like they are part of something bigger, a valuable piece of the puzzle that, when combined with others, creates a beautiful picture of success.

Balancing personalities, skills, and perspectives within a team is an art in itself. It involves recognizing and appreciating the diversity of your team members. People come with their own experiences, strengths, and working styles. The key is to harness this diversity, turning it into a strength rather than a source of conflict.

Understanding the personality traits of your team members can be immensely beneficial. Some individuals may be naturally extroverted and enjoy taking charge, while others might be introverted and excel in deep thinking and analysis. Recognizing these traits and assigning roles accordingly can foster a more harmonious working environment.

Diverse skill sets, as in the case of cross-functional teams, are akin to a variety of ingredients in a recipe. Each skill brings a unique flavor to the team's capabilities. It's essential to identify these skills and allocate tasks that play to each individual's strengths. For instance, a marketer and a data analyst can be paired up to collaborate on a campaign, combining creativity with data-driven insights. This cross-pollination of skills not only enhances the project's outcome but also creates an environment where team members learn from each other and expand their skill sets.

In addition to balancing skills, it's crucial to cultivate a culture of open communication. A team that communicates freely and openly is more likely to overcome challenges and make the most of their combined skills. Communication should be as natural as breathing, and every contribution should be valued. It's about creating an atmosphere where everyone feels comfortable sharing ideas, providing feedback, and expressing concerns.

To ensure open communication, regular meetings, brainstorming sessions, and one-on-one chats should be part of the team's routine. These interactions serve as forums for exchanging ideas and addressing concerns. They also reinforce the sense of belonging, ensuring that the team operates like a well-oiled machine.

As a leader, your role in this balancing act is pivotal. You need to act as the mediator when conflicts arise and the motivator when individuals face challenges. You should encourage and facilitate the sharing of ideas and foster an environment of mutual respect. This, in turn, promotes a sense of psychological safety where team members are unafraid to voice their thoughts and concerns.

As the conductor of collaboration, you should be the embodiment of the collaborative spirit. Your actions and behaviors set the tone for the entire team. Lead by example by being open to feedback, being willing to collaborate, and showing appreciation for each team member's contributions.

In building an effective and collaborative team, it's vital to recognize the profound benefits that emerge. Each team member stands to gain substantially from the experience. Just as each chef in the kitchen grows from shared culinary experiences, your team members flourish in the collaborative journey.

For example, junior team members can gain exposure to different areas of expertise through cross-functional collaboration. This not only broadens their skill set but also fuels personal growth and a sense of accomplishment. They begin to see how their work contributes to the bigger picture, which provides a sense of purpose and validation, fostering a positive and motivating atmosphere.

A collaborative team becomes a hub of innovation. Imagine a scenario where team members from diverse backgrounds collaborate to brainstorm solutions. Their combined perspectives lead to breakthrough ideas that would have been overlooked in a siloed environment. This culture of innovation not only boosts team morale but also propels the entire organization forward.

Team members also benefit from the vast pool of knowledge and skills present within the team. They have the opportunity to learn from each other, acquiring new competencies and broadening their horizons. Collaboration becomes a source of continuous learning and development, enriching the individual as well as the team.

A collaborative team is more likely to be engaged and satisfied in their work. The sense of belonging and the knowledge that their contributions are valued create a positive and motivating atmosphere. Team members derive a sense of achievement and fulfillment from their collaborative efforts.

The benefits of collaboration extend beyond the individual team members. The entire organization reaps the rewards of an innovative and high-performing team. The culture of innovation that emerges from a collaborative environment can lead to the development of groundbreaking products or services. Cross-functional collaboration often results in more efficient and effective solutions to complex problems, ultimately benefiting the organization's bottom line.

The art of creating a collaborative team is a multifaceted process that involves setting a clear vision, balancing personalities and skills, and fostering open communication. This collaborative environment offers a plethora of benefits to both individual team members and the organization as a whole.

Ingredients of Effective Collaboration

Effective collaboration is a cornerstone of success for any team, and it begins with recognizing and celebrating the unique contributions of each team member. Every individual brings their own distinct qualities and skills to the table, and these differences are what make a team diverse and versatile. To foster an environment of effective collaboration, it's essential to cultivate a space where ideas can flow freely, communication is seamless, and every contribution is valued.

One of the keys to promoting effective collaboration is encouraging cross-functional teamwork. Just as different ingredients enhance the complexity and flavor of a dish, diverse skills enrich your team's problem-solving capabilities. By structuring projects that require a wide range of skills and expertise, you create opportunities for team members to bring their unique talents to the forefront.

Viewing Each Team Member as a Unique Contributor

To build a culture of effective collaboration, it's vital to view each team member as a unique contributor. Recognize that every individual possesses their own strengths, experiences, and skills that are valuable to the team's overall success. By acknowledging and celebrating these differences, you create an environment where each team member feels seen and appreciated for what they bring to the table.

Consider a scenario where your team includes members with various backgrounds and expertise. For instance, you may have team members with marketing, data analysis, and design skills. Instead of expecting them to conform to a single mold, leverage their unique abilities to tackle complex challenges and create innovative solutions.

When team members are allowed to shine in their areas of expertise, it not only enhances their sense of purpose and belonging but also drives the team's collective success. For instance, a data analyst may excel in providing insights, while a designer may have a knack for creating visually appealing materials. By recognizing these talents and encouraging team members to contribute their unique strengths, you're empowering the team to tackle a wide range of tasks with greater effectiveness.

Fostering an Environment of Open Communication

Effective collaboration relies on the establishment of an environment where open communication is the norm. This involves creating a space where team members feel comfortable sharing ideas, providing feedback, and expressing concerns. In such an environment, communication becomes as natural as breathing, and every contribution is valued.

One way to foster open communication is by setting the tone as a leader. Be an active listener, encourage team members to speak up, and create a culture of mutual respect. As the leader, your actions set the example for the entire team. When team members witness your willingness to listen and consider their input, they're more likely to follow suit and engage in open communication.

In addition to your leadership, it's essential to establish regular channels for communication within the team. This could involve scheduling frequent team meetings, brainstorming sessions, and one-on-one discussions. These interactions serve as forums for sharing ideas, addressing concerns, and ensuring that everyone's voice is heard.

Creating a collaborative environment where team members feel safe and respected when sharing their thoughts and concerns not only strengthens the sense of belonging but also ensures that the team operates like a well-oiled machine. When everyone's input is valued, the team can collectively make more informed decisions and reach better outcomes.

Encouraging Cross-Functional Collaboration

Cross-functional collaboration is a powerful tool that can significantly enhance a team's problem-solving capabilities. It's akin to combining various ingredients to create a complex and delicious dish. By encouraging team members with diverse skills to work together on projects, you create an environment where multiple perspectives and expertise come together to tackle challenges.

Consider the scenario of a marketing expert and a data analyst working on a campaign. The marketing expert brings creativity and market insights to the table, while the data analyst provides data-driven insights and analysis. By combining these diverse skill sets, the team can create a well-rounded and effective campaign that resonates with the target audience.

Encouraging cross-functional collaboration not only leads to more innovative and comprehensive solutions but also fosters a learning environment. Team members can learn from each other and expand their skill sets by working on projects that require collaboration across different disciplines. This kind of professional growth can be highly motivating and rewarding for team members.

The building blocks of effective collaboration involve recognizing the unique contributions of each team member, fostering an environment of open communication, and encouraging cross-functional collaboration. When these elements are in place, the team can leverage its diverse skills and expertise to tackle challenges and create innovative solutions. Collaboration becomes the driving force behind a team's success, resulting in a more engaged and capable group that can tackle a wide range of tasks with confidence and effectiveness.

Unlocking the Abundant Benefits of Effective Team Collaboration

When team collaboration is effective, to provides a source of substantial rewards for individual team members. Just as individuals grow and develop from shared experiences, team members flourish in their collaborative journey. This journey is a catalyst for personal growth, skill enhancement, and innovation, fostering stronger bonds within the team and propelling the entire organization towards success.

Personal Growth and Skill Enhancement

Effective collaboration provides an environment ripe for the personal growth and skill enhancement of team members. Just as professionals in various fields expand their horizons through shared experiences, your team members have the opportunity to enrich their skill sets and knowledge during the collaborative process.

Consider a junior team member participating in cross-functional collaboration. By engaging with colleagues possessing diverse areas of expertise, they gain exposure to a broader range of knowledge and skills. This exposure not only broadens their professional horizons but also nurtures personal growth and a profound sense of accomplishment.

For instance, a junior team member collaborating with a seasoned data analyst can deepen their understanding of data-driven insights and analysis. This newfound knowledge can enhance their problem-solving abilities and contribute to their professional development. The junior team member not only broadens their skill set but also gains confidence in their abilities, fostering a sense of achievement and personal growth.

Acknowledging Unique Contributions

In a collaborative environment, team members come to recognize and appreciate the unique strengths and expertise that each individual brings to the table. Just as a diverse array of skills enriches a team's problem-solving capabilities, team members contribute their own distinctive qualities to the collective success.

In such an inclusive environment, team members not only acknowledge but celebrate the value of their contributions. This recognition fosters a positive and motivating atmosphere within the team. Team members experience a deep sense of purpose, knowing that their skills and expertise play a pivotal role in the team's success. This acknowledgment leads to personal fulfillment, heightened job satisfaction, and greater engagement in their work.

The Nexus of Innovation

Collaboration often transforms a team into a hub of innovation. Just as team members from various backgrounds come together to brainstorm solutions, the collective perspectives frequently lead to breakthrough ideas that might remain undiscovered in a more isolated working environment.

Imagine team members with diverse experiences and areas of expertise converging to address a complex problem. Their diverse viewpoints and approaches provide a rich tapestry of ideas and solutions. During the collaborative process, these individual insights intersect, creating an environment where innovation thrives.

In this culture of innovation, team members are encouraged to think creatively, challenge conventional approaches, and explore unconventional solutions. As a result, innovative ideas emerge, leading to more efficient processes, creative solutions, and groundbreaking products or services.

The culture of innovation not only boosts team morale but also propels the entire organization forward. When a collaborative team consistently generates innovative solutions, the organization gains a competitive edge in the marketplace. New products or services are developed, complex challenges are effectively addressed, and the organization's growth and success are accelerated.

The abundant benefits of effective team collaboration are numerous and far-reaching, benefiting both individual team members and the organization as a whole. Team members experience growth, skill enhancement, personal fulfillment, and a heightened sense of purpose. Collaboration also cultivates a culture of innovation that fuels organizational advancement.

The art of creating a harmonious and intentional team, marked by recognizing unique contributions, fostering open communication, and encouraging cross-functional collaboration, becomes the cornerstone of success. Collaboration serves as the driving force behind the team's unity and effectiveness, enabling them to confidently tackle a wide range of tasks and challenges with competence and efficiency.

Teammates 101: Getting to Know Your Superstars

Welcome to the vibrant classroom of connections and team experiences, where you're embarking on a journey to earn your degree in the art of Teammates 101. Envision yourself as a skilled detective, dedicated to uncovering the intricate layers of your team members' personalities, aspirations, and strengths. This treasure trove of knowledge isn't just a supplementary skill; it's the master key that unlocks your team's boundless potential and solidifies their loyalty.

The Heart-to-Heart Connection

Imagine each one-on-one conversation with your team members as a cherished heart-to-heart chat with a dear friend. These interactions delve beyond the surface, unearthing passions, dreams, and sources of enthusiasm. These discussions are your gateway to understanding the unique essence that each team member brings to the table.

To achieve this, embark on a journey of active listening and genuine interest. Engage your team members in discussions about their interests outside of work – their hobbies, their dreams, and what brings them joy. Discover what ignites their inner passion and motivation. As you delve into their personal stories, you're weaving a tapestry of connection that extends far beyond the confines of the workplace.

The Power of Understanding

Understanding your teammates goes beyond memorizing trivia about their preferences; it's about grasping the core elements that fuel their dedication and enthusiasm. Visualize this as decoding a language of inspiration unique to each individual.

To accomplish this, consider implementing "coffee chats" – informal one-on-one sessions where you discuss aspirations and career paths. Encourage team members to share their long-term goals, whether it's mastering a new skill, taking on leadership roles, or contributing to groundbreaking projects. As you gain insights into their ambitions, you're forging pathways for personalized growth within the team.

Unveiling Motivations for Excellence

Imagine understanding the secret ingredients that drive each team member to excel, just like a chef customizes a recipe to perfection. Unveiling these motivations is a gateway to unleashing unparalleled dedication and fostering team cohesion.

To make this a reality, consider periodic check-ins focused solely on career development. Inquire about their proudest accomplishments and the moments that ignited their passion for their work. By aligning their roles and tasks with their intrinsic motivations, you're crafting an environment where team members are driven to exceed expectations and create their best work.

Celebrating Diversity in Unity

Visualize your team as a vibrant mosaic, each piece representing a unique personality that contributes to the collective masterpiece. Embrace the beauty of diversity and create an environment where individuals are encouraged to express their authentic selves.

To achieve this, organize team-building activities that highlight each team member's distinct strengths. For example, host a "Skills Showcase" session where each member shares a skill or hobby outside of work. By celebrating their multifaceted talents, you're fostering a sense of belonging and pride in being part of a dynamic and diverse team.

Why It Matters: Team Cohesion and Loyalty

Understanding your superstars on a deeper level isn't just a charming notion; it's a strategic move that bolsters team cohesion and cultivates unwavering loyalty. As you forge connections beyond the surface, you're creating an atmosphere of mutual respect, where each member feels valued and seen.

Cohesion thrives when team members recognize each other's strengths and support one another's growth. By building these connections, you're nurturing an environment where collaboration flows seamlessly, innovation flourishes, and challenges are faced collectively. Teammates who feel genuinely understood and appreciated are more likely to invest their energy and commitment into the team's shared goals.

In essence, Teammates 101 isn't a mere introduction; it's a foundational course in fostering unity and loyalty. Just as a well-knit tapestry weaves individual threads into a breathtaking masterpiece, your efforts in understanding your superstars knit together a team that's bound by shared purpose and strengthened by the unique contributions of each member.

Goal Power: Charting a Course for Collective Success

Ahoy, captain of aspirations and navigator of achievement! You're standing at the helm, ready to set sail into the sea of goal power – a dynamic force that propels teams towards extraordinary accomplishments. Visualize yourself as the steadfast helmsman, steering your crew towards a shimmering destination that gleams on the horizon like a guiding light.

But let's be clear: goal power isn't about scribbling arbitrary targets on paper. It's about igniting a collective flame of purpose and determination that propels your team forward. Your role is to craft goals that are not merely SMART (Specific, Measurable, Achievable, Relevant, and Time-bound), but also infused with insight, inspiration and aspiration.

The Art of Goal Crafting: Painting the Future

Imagine goal crafting as an act of painting a vivid glance into the future – a future your team is eager and motivated to shape together. These goals are more than just bullet points; they become the engine driving your crew through trials and triumphs. And here's where the enchantment unfolds: as your team edges closer to these goals, the shared sense of achievement becomes a moment of oneness as a team, realizing what true potential they hold individually and together.

Unveiling SMART Goals: A Blueprint for Triumph

Now, let's delve deeper into the treasure chest of goal power and unearth the gems of SMART goals. These gems, when polished become the stepping stones to a remarkable accomplishments. Let's unravel each facet of the SMART framework and illuminate it with practical examples:

Specific: Specific goals are like finely chiseled sculptures that leave no room for ambiguity. Instead of setting a vague goal like "increase sales," craft it to be "increase monthly sales by 15% within the next quarter." Ensure your team members fully understand what the expectation is.

Measurable: Measurable goals ensure that your crew can gauge success. For instance, instead of stating "improve customer satisfaction," make it "achieve a customer satisfaction rating of 90% or above on post-purchase surveys." Ensuring the goal is measurable is tantamount to success.

Achievable: Think of your goal as a mountain peak; it should be challenging but reachable. Instead of aiming to "dominate the market within a month," set the goal to "gain a 10% increase in market share over the next six months through targeted marketing campaigns." Work with your team and be sure they believe that it is achievable. If they do not think it is possible, your team can become frustrated and give up without trying.

Relevant: Envision your goal as a puzzle piece that seamlessly fits into the bigger picture. A relevant goal aligns with the mission, overarching strategy, broader objectives, priorities, and strategic direction of the team and organization. A relevant goal should directly contribute to the overall mission or purpose, and it should make sense within the larger context. For example, instead of pursuing a goal like "launch a new product line," make it "launch a new eco-friendly product line in alignment with our sustainability initiatives."

Time-Bound: Time-bound goals have a set timeframe that creates a sense of accountability. Transform "improve employee training" into "implement a comprehensive employee training program by the end of the quarter."

Embarking on Goal Achievement: Setting the Course

Crafting SMART goals is just the first leg of the journey. Now, it's time to set the sails and steer your crew towards achievement:

Collaborative Goal Setting: Gather your team members and collaboratively set goals that resonate with each individual's strengths and aspirations. By involving everyone in the process, you create a sense of ownership and commitment.

Break Down and Conquer: Divide larger goals into smaller, manageable tasks. Just as a ship navigates through rough waters by tackling one wave at a time, your team can conquer complex goals by breaking them into actionable steps.

Regular Progress Checkpoints: Regularly track progress and celebrate milestones. Use progress reports, team meetings, or visual charts to keep everyone aligned and motivated.

Adapt and Evolve: Be open to adjusting your course based on changing circumstances. Encourage your team to share insights and suggest adaptations as needed.

Positive Reinforcement: Offer positive feedback and acknowledgment as your team makes progress. Celebrate achievements and highlight the collective effort.

Reflection and Learning: After achieving a goal, gather your team to reflect on what worked well and areas for improvement. This not only fosters continuous improvement but also strengthens team cohesion.

As your crew journeys towards the shores of achievement, remember that goal power is a dynamic force that unites your team's aspirations, fuels their determination, and solidifies their bond. Just as a ship's compass guides it to its destination, your skill in crafting and achieving SMART goals navigates your team towards greatness.

Strengths Galore: Unleash the Superpowers!

Picture each team member as a unique gem, radiating a distinctive brilliance that has the potential to light up the entire room. Your role, as the leader, is akin to that of a skilled gemologist, diligently identifying and nurturing these strengths until they shine. However, it's not just about the individual brilliance; it's about harnessing these strengths to achieve team excellence and synergy.

Combining strengths can be compared to assembling a set of unique gears, carefully intertwining them to ensure that each complements the other flawlessly. In the same vein, there's an art to recognizing complementary strengths, strategically pairing team members, and witnessing the dynamic bursts of extraordinary that occur when these strengths come together.

Unleashing strengths goes beyond mere task assignment; it involves aligning roles with passions, skills, and untapped potential. When team members operate within their strengths zone, they are not merely productive; they become unstoppable forces of innovation and creativity. As a leader, you possess the ability to unlock these superpowers, transforming your team into a league of extraordinary individuals.

As you navigate the vibrant landscape of team dynamics, remember that each interaction, each goal set, and each strength harnessed contributes to the symphony of success echoing throughout your team's journey.

Understanding the Gems Within Your Team

In the world of effective leadership, recognizing the unique strengths and talents of each team member is a fundamental task. It's akin to being a gemologist who carefully inspects, cleans, and polishes precious stones to reveal their full brilliance. Similarly, as a leader, your role involves identifying the inherent strengths of your team members and honing them to perfection.

Each team member possesses their own set of strengths, which can include technical skills, soft skills, creative talents, or personal attributes. Some may excel in problem-solving, others in communication, and some may exhibit strong leadership qualities. It's essential to understand that these strengths are not limited to job-related skills but encompass the full spectrum of abilities that individuals bring to the table.

To unlock the superpowers within your team, it's imperative to conduct a thorough assessment of these strengths. This can be achieved through self-assessment, peer evaluations, or professional assessments. The goal is to compile a comprehensive inventory of each team member's strengths and align them with the team's objectives and goals.

The Art of Complementary Strengths

Unleashing the superpowers within your team involves more than just recognizing individual strengths; it's about strategically combining these strengths for maximum impact. Think of it as assembling a complex puzzle where each piece fits seamlessly with the others. This concept is rooted in the idea of complementary strengths.

Complementary strengths are those that naturally pair well with one another, creating a harmonious and highly effective team dynamic. For instance, if one team member excels in analytical thinking while another possesses exceptional creativity, combining their strengths can lead to innovative problem-solving solutions. Likewise, if someone is highly organized and detail-oriented, they can complement a team member with strong leadership skills who may excel in vision-setting and strategic thinking.

Identifying these complementary strengths is a nuanced art that requires a deep understanding of your team members and their capabilities. It involves observing team dynamics, conducting team assessments, and fostering open communication within the team. By aligning individuals with complementary strengths, you not only harness their superpowers but also enhance their ability to work cohesively and effectively towards shared goals.

Aligning Roles with Passions and Strengths

Effective leadership isn't just about recognizing and combining strengths; it's also about aligning roles with the passions, skills, and untapped potential of your team members. When individuals are allowed to work in areas that resonate with their strengths, they not only perform at their best but also find a deep sense of fulfillment and purpose in their work.

To achieve this alignment, it's essential to conduct in-depth discussions with team members, exploring their aspirations, career goals, and areas of interest. This can be achieved through one-on-one meetings, performance evaluations, or regular check-ins. By understanding what drives and motivates each team member, you can strategically assign tasks and projects that align with their passions and strengths.

For example, if a team member is highly skilled in client communication and has a passion for relationship-building, consider assigning them roles that involve client engagement and account management. This not only leverages their strengths but also increases their job satisfaction and motivation.

In a collaborative environment where roles are aligned with individual strengths and passions, team members are not merely productive; they become highly engaged and inspired. They bring their best selves to work, consistently deliver exceptional results, and contribute to the overall success of the team.

Becoming the Strength Whisperer

As a leader, you hold the wand that can unleash the superpowers of your team, turning them into a league of extraordinary individuals. This role can be likened to that of a "Strength Whisperer" who has the ability to recognize, nurture, and amplify the strengths within each team member.

To become an effective Strength Whisperer, there are several key strategies to employ:

Active Listening: Take the time to actively listen to your team members. Encourage open and honest conversations where they can share their aspirations, challenges, and areas where they believe their strengths shine. By being an attentive listener, you can gain valuable insights into their individual strengths and how they perceive their roles within the team.

Feedback and Recognition: Provide regular feedback and recognition to your team members. Acknowledge their contributions, highlight their strengths, and express appreciation for their efforts. Recognition serves as a motivator and encourages team members to continue leveraging their strengths.

Empowerment: Empower your team members by giving them autonomy and trust to make decisions within their strengths zone. This not only fosters a sense of ownership but also allows them to fully utilize their superpowers to achieve team goals.

Coaching and Development: Offer opportunities for coaching and development to help team members further hone their strengths. Provide access to resources, training, and mentorship to support their growth and skill enhancement.

Adaptability: Be flexible and adaptable in your leadership approach. Recognize that individuals' strengths may evolve over time, and be willing to adjust roles and responsibilities accordingly.

Collaboration: Encourage collaboration within the team, fostering an environment where team members can learn from one another and share their strengths. Collaborative projects provide opportunities for complementary strengths to shine and for the team as a whole to achieve exceptional results.

As you navigate the path of a Strength Whisperer, you'll witness the transformation of your team into a harmonious orchestra of collective brilliance. Each interaction, each goal set, and each strength harnessed contributes to the symphony of success that echoes throughout your team's journey.

The Power of Recognition and Feedback

One of the fundamental tools in unleashing the superpowers of your team is the power of recognition and feedback. Just as a skilled gemologist knows the importance of acknowledging and celebrating the beauty of each gem, you, as a leader, must recognize and appreciate the unique strengths and contributions of your team members.

Recognition is a potent motivator that reinforces positive behaviors and encourages team members to continue leveraging their strengths. It not only boosts morale but also instills a sense of accomplishment and belonging within the team. Regular recognition creates a positive and motivating atmosphere that enhances job satisfaction.

Stay tuned as we continue our expedition through the heartwarming principles of leadership!

Chapter 3

Unleash Your Inner Captain

Ahoy, captain of the ship of progress! In this captivating chapter, we're setting sail on an extraordinary voyage into the heart of leadership mastery. As you embrace the role of captain, you'll navigate the waters of delegation mastery, empower your crew through shared decision-making, amplify your team's skills to new heights, and cultivate a culture of perpetual growth. So, prepare to chart a course through uncharted leadership territories, don your captain's hat, and let the adventure begin!

Jedi Master of Delegation (Almost!)

Imagine stepping into the shoes of a Jedi master of delegation, harnessing the mystical power of balance and wisdom to expertly distribute responsibilities and tasks. Delegation isn't merely a matter of offloading assignments; it's an artful dance of entrusting the right responsibilities to the right team members, ensuring optimal efficiency, productivity, and development.

Think of your team as a fleet of starships, each with its unique strengths and capabilities. Just as a Jedi carefully selects the appropriate lightsaber for each battle, you'll learn to assess your team members' strengths, skills, and expertise, assigning tasks that align with their abilities. But this isn't about relinquishing control; it's about sharing it in a way that fosters collaboration, innovation, and growth.

Mastering delegation involves trust to empower your team members to take the lead in their designated areas. As you pass the baton of responsibility, you're fostering a sense of ownership and accountability that propels your team toward greatness. Your leadership becomes a guiding force, steering the ship toward collective success while allowing individual talents to shine.

Delegation for Team Success: A Strategic Approach

Effective delegation is a cornerstone of successful leadership. It involves recognizing the skills and expertise within your team and entrusting tasks to individuals who are best equipped to handle them. This strategic approach to delegation not only maximizes efficiency but also fosters team growth and success.

In the world of leadership and team management, delegation is a powerful tool that can significantly impact productivity, innovation, and job satisfaction. It's the process of assigning tasks and responsibilities to team members based on their individual skills, expertise, and strengths. When done effectively, delegation can lead to exceptional outcomes, as it ensures that each task is tackled by the most qualified team member.

This strategic approach to delegation is akin to assembling a puzzle, where each piece fits perfectly into place. It's about recognizing that your team is composed of individuals with distinct capabilities and then matching tasks to the right individuals. Let's explore this concept further and delve into the art of delegation based on skills and expertise.

Understanding the Power of Delegation

Delegation is more than just a task distribution; it's a strategy for optimizing team performance. When you delegate tasks to team members who possess the necessary skills and expertise, you're essentially empowering them to take ownership and contribute to the team's success.

In practice, effective delegation has several key benefits:

1. Improved Efficiency: Tasks are completed more efficiently and accurately when assigned to individuals with the right skills. This reduces the risk of errors and ensures that deadlines are met.
2. Skill Utilization: Delegation allows you to harness the full potential of your team's skills and expertise. It enables team

members to perform tasks that align with their strengths and interests.

3. Development Opportunities: Delegation provides team members with opportunities to learn and grow. When they take on tasks that challenge and engage them, they develop new skills and gain valuable experience.
4. Enhanced Job Satisfaction: Team members who are delegated tasks that align with their skills and interests tend to experience greater job satisfaction. They feel valued and recognized for their contributions.
5. Effective Resource Allocation: By delegating tasks to the most qualified team members, you make efficient use of your team's resources. This allows you to focus on higher-priority activities that require your expertise.

The Art of Delegation Based on Skills and Expertise

Effective delegation begins with a deep understanding of your team's skills and expertise. It's essential to recognize the unique strengths and capabilities of each team member. Think of your team as a diverse toolbox, with each member representing a different tool. Your role as a leader is to ensure that each task is assigned to the right tool for the job.

Here are key steps to master the art of delegation based on skills and expertise:

1. Skill Assessment: Start by conducting a comprehensive assessment of your team members' skills and expertise. This can be achieved through self-assessment, performance evaluations, or one-on-one discussions.
2. Task Analysis: Break down tasks and responsibilities into their component parts. Understand the specific skills and knowledge required to complete each task effectively.
3. Task Matching: Match tasks to team members based on their skills and expertise. Consider not only their technical skills but also their personal attributes, such as problem-solving abilities, communication skills, and leadership qualities.
4. Clear Communication: When delegating a task, communicate your expectations clearly. Provide detailed instructions, set goals, and define the desired outcomes. Make sure team

members understand the task's importance and how it contributes to the team's goals.

5. Support and Resources: Ensure that team members have the necessary resources, tools, and support to complete the task successfully. This may include access to relevant information, training, or collaboration with other team members.

6. Empowerment: Encourage team members to take ownership of their delegated tasks. Empower them to make decisions and exercise their expertise while keeping you updated on their progress.

7. Regular Feedback: Maintain open lines of communication and provide feedback on delegated tasks. Acknowledge and appreciate the efforts and results of team members. This fosters a positive and motivating atmosphere within the team.

The Importance of Trust

Trust is a fundamental element of effective delegation. When you delegate tasks to team members based on their skills and expertise, you demonstrate trust in their abilities. This trust not only motivates team members but also boosts their confidence and job satisfaction.

To build trust within your team, consider the following principles:

1. Open Communication: Foster a culture of open communication where team members feel comfortable discussing their skills, strengths, and areas for development. Encourage them to express their interests and career aspirations.

2. Respect for Expertise: Recognize and respect the expertise and knowledge that each team member brings to the table. This acknowledgement validates their contributions and fosters a sense of pride in their work.

3. Recognition and Appreciation: Regularly recognize and appreciate the efforts of team members. Acknowledge their accomplishments, no matter how small, and express gratitude for their contributions.

4. Support and Development: Provide opportunities for skill development and growth. Offer access to training, mentorship, and resources that enable team members to further enhance their expertise.

The Role of Leadership in Delegation

As a leader, your role in delegation goes beyond task assignment. You serve as a facilitator of growth and success within your team. Here are some key aspects of your role in effective delegation:

1. Strategic Planning: Develop a strategic plan for task delegation based on the team's objectives and goals. Prioritize tasks and match them to team members with the requisite skills.
2. Clear Direction: Ensure that team members have a clear understanding of their delegated tasks, including goals, deadlines, and expected outcomes. Address any questions or concerns promptly.
3. Empowerment: Empower team members to make decisions and take ownership of their tasks. Encourage them to utilize their expertise and problem-solving skills to overcome challenges.
4. Monitoring and Feedback: Regularly monitor the progress of delegated tasks and provide constructive feedback. Recognize and appreciate the achievements of team members, reinforcing their sense of purpose and job satisfaction.
5. Adaptability: Be flexible in your approach to delegation. Recognize that skills and strengths may evolve over time and be willing to adjust roles and responsibilities accordingly.
6. Continuous Improvement: Continuously assess and refine your delegation strategies. Identify areas for improvement and provide opportunities for team members to expand their skills and expertise.

Incorporating Delegation into Leadership

Delegation based on skills and expertise is a dynamic process that evolves with the team's growth and changing priorities. It's a leadership skill that requires continuous refinement and adaptability. Here are some tips on incorporating effective delegation into your leadership style:

1. Set Clear Expectations: Clearly define the expectations, responsibilities, and goals associated with each delegated task. This ensures that team members have a complete understanding of their roles.

2. Provide Autonomy: Allow team members the autonomy to make decisions and take ownership of their tasks. Empowering them to use their expertise promotes engagement and innovation.
3. Monitor Progress: Regularly check in on the progress of delegated tasks. Offer guidance, support, and feedback to help team members succeed.
4. Recognize Achievements: Recognize and celebrate the achievements of team members who excel in their delegated roles. This not only boosts morale but also reinforces their sense of purpose.
5. Adapt and Adjust: Be willing to adapt and adjust your delegation strategies as the team evolves. Recognize that individuals' skills and strengths may change over time.
6. Encourage Development: Offer opportunities for skill development and growth. Encourage team members to explore new areas of expertise and expand their skill sets.
7. Foster a Collaborative Environment: Create a collaborative environment where team members can share their expertise and learn from one another. Collaboration enhances the collective knowledge and skills of the team.

Delegation is a vital leadership skill that contributes to team success and individual growth. When tasks are assigned based on skills and expertise, team members are more engaged, productive, and satisfied in their roles. It's a win-win approach that benefits both the team and the organization.

Incorporating delegation into your leadership style not only optimizes team performance but also creates a culture of trust, growth, and success. It's a powerful tool that empowers your team members to shine and allows you, as a leader, to focus on higher-priority activities, driving the team and the organization forward.

The Importance of Delegation:

Delegation isn't just a management tactic; it's a leadership philosophy with profound implications:

1. Skill Development: Delegation offers team members opportunities to develop new skills and expand their

capabilities. When you delegate tasks that challenge and stretch their abilities, you're fostering a culture of continuous learning and growth.

2. Building Future Leaders: Effective delegation is a cornerstone of leadership development. As you entrust responsibilities to your team, you're grooming them for future leadership roles. You're creating a pipeline of capable leaders who can guide the ship when needed.

3. Optimizing Efficiency: Delegation optimizes your team's efficiency. By matching tasks with the right individuals, you're ensuring that each task is tackled by someone with the required skills, leading to quicker and more accurate results.

4. Fostering Collaboration: Delegation encourages collaboration. When team members work together on delegated tasks, they share knowledge, ideas, and perspectives, enhancing the quality of the outcome.

Empowering Through Delegation

In essence, delegation isn't a loss of control; it's a strategic move to distribute responsibility and foster growth. By recognizing your team's unique strengths and empowering them through delegation, you not only ensure tasks are completed efficiently but also mold future leaders who can confidently navigate the challenges ahead.

The Delegation Blueprint

Now, let's dive into the practicalities of delegation, crafting your personalized delegation blueprint:

Know Your Team's Strengths:

Take time to understand your team members' strengths, skills, and expertise. What are their superpowers? What tasks align with their abilities?

Example: If you have a team member with exceptional project management skills, entrust them with overseeing complex projects. This plays to their strengths and frees up your time for higher-level strategic planning.

Set Clear Expectations:

When delegating, provide crystal-clear instructions and expectations while giving them latitude to perform the task in their own way. Define the task's objectives, deadlines, and desired outcomes.

Example: If you're delegating a research task, specify the key questions to be answered, the sources to consult, and the deadline for completion.

Offer Support and Resources:

Ensure your team members have the necessary resources, tools, and support to complete their tasks successfully. This might include access to specific software, training, or mentorship.

Example: If a team member is tasked with creating a presentation, ensure they have access to design software and offer guidance or feedback if needed.

Maintain Open Communication:

Foster a culture of open communication where team members feel comfortable asking questions or seeking clarification. Regularly check in on progress without micromanaging.

Example: Schedule brief check-in meetings to discuss progress, address any challenges, and provide guidance if necessary.

Acknowledge and Appreciate:

Recognize and appreciate your team members' efforts throughout the duration of the task timeline. Acknowledge their achievements and the impact of their work. This not only boosts morale but also reinforces a sense of ownership.

Example: In team meetings or one-on-one discussions, publicly commend team members for their contributions and the positive outcomes achieved through delegation.

Feedback Loop:

After task completion, engage in a feedback loop. Discuss what went well, what could be improved, and how the team member feels about the experience. Use this feedback to refine your future delegation strategies.

Example: Sit down with the team member to review the project they managed. Celebrate successes and discuss any challenges faced, offering guidance for improvement.

By following this delegation blueprint, you'll not only ensure tasks are handled efficiently but also empower your team members to develop their skills, take on greater responsibilities, and ultimately become future leaders. Remember, effective delegation is a Jedi-level skill that propels your team toward greatness while nurturing individual growth and potential. May the force of delegation be with you!

Pass the Torch: Sharing Decision-Making Magic

Shared decision-making is a powerful approach to leadership that empowers team members to take an active role in shaping the direction of their collective efforts. It's a cultural shift that values and embraces the voices and insights of every team member in the process of decision-making. In this realm, synergy is the dynamic that arises when diverse perspectives converge to create innovative solutions. As a leader, your role is to step back, allowing your team members to combine their ideas, fostering energy and excitement as they envision the goal as not just attainable but fully owned.

Shared decision-making isn't about making decisions by committee, but rather, it's about creating a culture where individuals feel valued, empowered, and confident in their contributions. Each team member becomes a stakeholder in the journey, fully invested in the destination and the path taken to reach it. As you guide your team through this landscape, you're not just empowering them; you're igniting a sense of ownership and commitment that can be life-changing for your team members. The decisions made become a collective blend of expertise, creativity, and collaboration, leading to stronger team cohesion and better outcomes.

The Essence of Shared Decision-Making

Shared decision-making is a philosophy and practice that shifts the traditional top-down approach to leadership. Instead of a single decision-maker at the helm, it recognizes that the combined wisdom and diverse perspectives of the team can often lead to better decisions and more successful outcomes.

At its core, shared decision-making involves inclusivity, collaboration, empowerment, consensus building, transparency, and accountability. It ensures that every team member has a seat at the decision-making table, regardless of rank or role. It encourages open communication and collaboration among team members, where ideas are freely exchanged, and the decision-making process is transparent. Team members are empowered to contribute their insights and ideas, fostering a sense of ownership and responsibility for the outcomes.

The Benefits of Shared Decision-Making

Shared decision-making offers a multitude of benefits for both the team and the organization as a whole. These benefits extend to various aspects of team dynamics and performance, including enhanced team engagement, diverse perspectives, improved communication, strengthened trust, higher job satisfaction, effective problem-solving, ownership and accountability, faster implementation, and adaptability to changing circumstances.

Incorporating Shared Decision-Making

Implementing shared decision-making in your team requires a thoughtful approach and a commitment to a more inclusive and collaborative work environment. Assess the existing culture within your team and organization to understand the current decision-making processes and the extent to which team members are involved.

Educate and train team members on the concept of shared decision-making and its benefits. Provide training on effective communication and collaborative problem-solving. Define the scope of shared decision-making within your team, clarifying which types of decisions will involve team members and to what extent.

Create structured processes for shared decision-making, which may involve regular team meetings, brainstorming sessions, or decision-making committees. Foster an environment where team members feel safe to share their thoughts and ideas, encouraging open and respectful communication.

Equip your team with the tools and resources they need to participate effectively in decision-making. Act as a facilitator during decision-making discussions, ensuring that each team member has the opportunity to contribute, and guide the conversation toward consensus when needed. Celebrate the successes that result from shared decision-making and acknowledge the contributions of team members and the positive outcomes that emerge.

The Role of Leadership in Shared Decision-Making

Leaders play a pivotal role in fostering shared decision-making within their teams. As a leader, your actions and behaviors set the tone for the team's culture and approach to decision-making. Lead by example by actively involving team members in important decisions and valuing their perspectives.

Empower team members to make decisions within their areas of expertise and encourage them to take the initiative and trust their judgment. Provide guidance when needed, as your experience and insights can steer the team in the right direction. Create opportunities for team members to collaborate and share their ideas, and facilitate discussions while encouraging open communication.

Acknowledge and celebrate the contributions of team members in the decision-making process, showing appreciation for their efforts and insights. Be open to feedback from your team regarding the shared decision-making process and use this feedback to make improvements and enhance the overall experience.

Incorporating shared decision-making into your leadership style can have a profound impact on your team's effectiveness, engagement, and innovation. It's a shift from the traditional top-down approach to a collaborative and inclusive model where team members are co-captains of the journey, fully engaged and invested in the path to success.

Skill Up: Pumping Up Your Team's Muscles

Welcome to the role of a visionary coach, a nurturing mentor, and a sculptor of expertise. As you set forth on this expedition, your mission is to elevate your team's skills to unprecedented heights. Envision yourself as a master craftsman, shaping raw potential into refined prowess, much like an artisan molds clay into a piece of beautiful art.

Customized Training: Nurturing Individual Flourish

Imagine your team members as a collection of raw gems, each possessing unique facets that shine with potential. Your task resembles that of a skilled lapidary, shaping and polishing these gems to reveal their dazzling brilliance. Just as a personal trainer tailors workouts to an athlete's needs, you'll curate experiences that empower your team members to become experts in their respective domains.

Begin by conducting a skill assessment for each team member. Identify their strengths, pinpoint areas for improvement, and uncover latent talents. For instance, if a team member excels in project management but seeks to enhance their communication skills, you could design a training plan focused on effective communication strategies.

Crafting the Training Regimen: A Spectrum of Learning

Crafting a dynamic training regimen requires strategic finesse. Visualize yourself as an architect, designing a structure that nurtures growth and fosters skill refinement. Utilize a spectrum of learning methods to cater to diverse learning styles:

Workshops and Webinars: Organize interactive workshops or invite industry experts for webinars. These sessions expose your team to the latest trends, tools, and best practices. For example, if your team is in digital marketing, a workshop on social media algorithms could enhance their expertise.

Mentorship Programs: Establish mentorship pairings between seasoned and junior team members. This symbiotic relationship facilitates knowledge transfer, offering valuable insights and guidance. A senior graphic designer could mentor a junior designer, sharing design principles and software techniques.

Cross-Functional Experiences: Encourage team members to venture beyond their comfort zones. Assign projects that require collaboration across departments. If you're in software development, a developer could collaborate with the user experience team to gain insights into user-centric design.

Skill-Enhancing Challenges: Create internal challenges that stimulate innovation and creativity. For instance, challenge your team to develop a creative marketing campaign for a fictional product, fostering imaginative thinking and campaign planning.

Continuous Learning Platforms: Invest in online courses or platforms tailored to skill enhancement. Platforms like Coursera or LinkedIn Learning offer a plethora of courses, from data analysis to leadership skills.

Fostering a Culture of Learning: Growth as a Lifestyle

Beyond training, instill a culture that values continuous learning and celebrates skill. development. Foster an environment where team members share insights, discuss learnings, and collectively elevate the team's expertise.

Hold regular "Knowledge Sharing" sessions where team members present on topics they've learned. Encourage peer feedback and discussions, fostering an atmosphere of mutual support and learning. Establish a "Skill of the Month" initiative, where each month focuses on developing a specific skill, allowing team members to collaborate and learn together.

In the fast-paced and ever-evolving landscape of today's professional world, the concept of continuous learning has shifted from a choice to a necessity. It's no longer enough to rely solely on formal training programs; organizations must cultivate a culture where learning is deeply embedded in the team's DNA. This is where fostering a culture of learning comes into play, emphasizing growth as a lifestyle rather than a sporadic event.

Why is a Culture of Learning Important?

Before we delve into the specifics of how to foster such a culture, let's underscore the significance of embracing continuous learning as a fundamental organizational value. A culture of learning offers several compelling advantages:

Adaptability: In a rapidly changing business environment, adaptability is key. A culture of learning ensures that your team is prepared to embrace new technologies, methodologies, and strategies as they emerge.

Innovation: Learning fosters creativity and innovation. When team members are encouraged to explore new ideas and expand their horizons, they are more likely to come up with fresh, groundbreaking solutions.

Employee Engagement: Learning opportunities boost employee engagement and satisfaction. Team members appreciate organizations that invest in their growth, leading to increased retention and motivation.

Skill Enhancement: Continuous learning allows team members to sharpen their existing skills and acquire new ones. This is vital for staying competitive in the job market and within your industry.

Knowledge Sharing: A culture of learning promotes knowledge sharing. When team members are actively encouraged to share insights and learn from one another, the collective intelligence of the group grows exponentially.

Now, let's explore how to transform these principles into actionable strategies.

Regular "Knowledge Sharing" Initiative:

Imagine a scenario where your team members gather regularly to share knowledge, insights, and discoveries. These sessions are not just about presenting polished reports but about creating an environment where open dialogue and knowledge exchange are the norm.

How to Implement Knowledge Sharing Sessions:

Frequency: Set a regular schedule for these sessions. Monthly or bi-monthly meetings work well. Consistency is key.

Volunteer-Based: Encourage team members to volunteer to present on topics they've learned or explored recently. This could be related to their work or even personal interests if they have relevance to the team.

Open Discussions: After each presentation, foster open discussions where team members can ask questions, share their own experiences, and offer suggestions for improvement.

Peer Feedback: Encourage constructive peer feedback. Team members can provide feedback on the presentation style, content, and its applicability to the team's goals.

Knowledge Repository: Create a repository or database where session materials, such as presentation slides or notes, are stored for future reference.

"Skill of the Month" Initiative:

The "Skill of the Month" program is an excellent example of a structured initiative. Each month, the team focuses on developing a specific skill or competency.

How to Implement the "Skill of the Month" Initiative:

Skill Selection: At the start of each month, select a skill or competency relevant to the team's objectives. Consider input from team members to ensure that the chosen skill aligns with their needs and interests.

Learning Resources: Provide team members with access to resources related to the selected skill. This could include articles, books, online courses, or in-house training sessions.

Practice and Application: Encourage team members to actively practice and apply the skill in their daily tasks and projects. This hands-on experience is crucial for skill mastery.

Collaboration: Foster a sense of collaboration by encouraging team members to work together on skill development. Peer learning is often highly effective.

Progress Tracking: Implement a system for tracking individual and collective progress in developing the skill of the month. Celebrate milestones and achievements.

Peer Feedback and Discussions:

Learning doesn't happen in isolation. It thrives in an environment where team members can openly discuss their experiences, ask questions, and provide feedback to one another.

How to Facilitate Peer Feedback and Discussions:

Communication Channels: Establish communication channels or forums where team members can engage in discussions related to their learning journeys. This could be through team meetings, dedicated chat groups, or online platforms.

Feedback Guidelines: Provide guidelines for offering constructive feedback. Encourage team members to focus on the positive aspects of their peers' efforts while also suggesting areas for improvement.

Mentorship: Consider implementing a mentorship program where more experienced team members can guide and support those who are working on specific skills.

Learning Communities: Encourage the formation of smaller learning communities or study groups within the team. These communities can focus on particular topics or skills, allowing for deeper exploration.

Creating a Learning Resources Hub:

To truly embrace continuous learning, it's essential to provide easy access to a wealth of learning resources. Establishing a centralized hub for such resources can be immensely beneficial.

How to Create a Learning Resources Hub:

Digital Platform: Develop a digital platform or use existing collaboration tools where team members can access recommended learning materials. Organize these resources by skill, topic, or difficulty level.

Resource Recommendations: Invite team members to recommend valuable resources they've discovered. Encourage them to share why these resources were helpful.

Feedback Loop: Create a feedback loop where team members can rate and review learning materials. This helps in curating the most relevant and effective resources.

Regular Updates: Ensure that the hub is regularly updated with new materials, keeping it fresh and relevant to the team's evolving needs.

Learning Goals and Progress Tracking:

Individualized learning goals and progress tracking are instrumental in making continuous learning a reality. When team members set goals and see their progress, they're more likely to stay motivated.

How to Implement Learning Goals and Progress Tracking:

Goal Setting: Encourage team members to set specific learning goals. These goals should be tied to the skills or competencies they wish to develop.

Regular Check-Ins: Hold regular one-on-one or group check-ins where team members can discuss their learning goals and progress. Use these sessions to offer support, guidance, and resources as needed.

Milestone Celebrations: Celebrate milestones and achievements, whether they're related to completing a course, mastering a skill, or applying new knowledge effectively in a project.

Feedback and Adjustments: Encourage team members to seek feedback on their progress. If they encounter challenges or obstacles, help them adjust their learning strategies.

Recognition and Celebration:

Recognition is a powerful motivator. Acknowledging and celebrating individual and collective achievements in learning and skill development reinforces the value of continuous improvement.

How to Implement Recognition and Celebration:

Recognition Programs: Integrate learning and skill development milestones into your team's recognition and rewards program. This could include certificates, badges, or public recognition during team meetings.

Success Stories: Showcase success stories within the team. Highlight individuals who have made significant strides in their growth journey, and allow them to share their experiences and insights.

Team Celebrations: Host team celebrations or events to mark significant learning milestones. This can create a sense of camaraderie and motivation.

The Power of a Learning Culture

Fostering a culture of learning that values continuous growth as a lifestyle is a transformative journey. It requires commitment, resources, and a collective mindset dedicated to improvement. By implementing the strategies outlined here, you'll not only elevate your team's expertise but also nurture an environment where curiosity, innovation, and adaptability thrive. In this culture of learning, your team members become not only better professionals but also more fulfilled individuals on their own growth journeys. It's a win-win scenario that propels both your team and your organization toward a brighter future.

The Blossoming Evolution: Nurturing Lifelong Growth

As a leader, your role in guiding your team is akin to witnessing a transformation, much like the metamorphosis of a caterpillar into a butterfly. You have the opportunity to observe your team members as they evolve into confident, adept, and multi-faceted professionals, ready to conquer challenges and soar to new heights.

The journey towards fostering skill development and growth within your team goes beyond immediate gains. It involves nurturing an environment of continuous learning and expertise. This commitment not only benefits the present but also lays the foundation for a legacy of lifelong learning. The accomplishments of your team will stand as a testament to your leadership acumen – a legacy that reverberates through their careers and contributes to the enduring success of the organization.

The Transformation Process

Much like the stages of a caterpillar's transformation into a butterfly, the evolution of your team members is a multi-step process. It begins with recognizing the potential for growth and development within each individual. Just as a caterpillar possesses the genetic code for becoming a butterfly, your team members harbor unique talents, skills, and potential that can be harnessed and cultivated.

The process involves providing the right conditions for growth and learning. This includes access to resources, opportunities for skill development, and a supportive and encouraging environment. Just as a caterpillar requires the right environment to spin its cocoon and undergo metamorphosis, your team needs the right ecosystem to foster their growth.

Empowerment and Encouragement

One of your primary roles as a leader is to empower and encourage your team members to take ownership of their own growth and development. Much like the caterpillar's instinct to spin its cocoon, your team members need the autonomy to make decisions, set goals, and pursue their own learning paths.

Empowerment also involves providing the necessary tools and resources to support skill development. Just as a caterpillar relies on its innate abilities and instincts, your team members need access to training, mentorship, and learning opportunities to aid their growth.

In addition to empowerment, encouragement plays a crucial role in the transformation process. Just as the caterpillar's transition into a pupa is a vulnerable stage, your team members may face challenges and doubts during their growth journey. It's your role to offer support, motivation, and positive reinforcement to help them overcome obstacles and continue their development.

Nurturing Lifelong Learning

The evolution of your team members into confident and multi-faceted professionals is not a one-time event. It's an ongoing journey that extends beyond their current roles and responsibilities. As a leader, you have the privilege of contributing to a legacy of lifelong learning within your team.

Encourage your team members to adopt a growth mindset, where they see challenges and setbacks as opportunities for learning and improvement. Just as a butterfly continuously adapts to its environment, your team members should be adaptable and open to new experiences and challenges.

Provide access to learning resources and opportunities that extend beyond their current roles. This may involve cross-training, mentoring, workshops, and further education. Support their pursuit of knowledge and expertise in areas that align with their interests and career aspirations.

Celebrate Achievements

Just as the emergence of a butterfly from its cocoon is a momentous occasion, celebrate the achievements and milestones of your team members. Acknowledge their growth and development and recognize their dedication and hard work.

Recognition and appreciation play a crucial role in motivating and inspiring your team members to continue their growth journey. When they feel valued and appreciated for their efforts, they are more likely to remain committed to their own development and contribute to the organization's success.

Institutionalizing a Culture of Growth

As a leader, your influence extends beyond individual team members; it encompasses the organization's culture as a whole. It's your responsibility to institutionalize a culture of growth and skill development that permeates every aspect of the workplace.

This involves setting clear expectations for continuous learning and skill development. Just as the caterpillar undergoes a transformation according to its innate instincts, your team should understand the organization's expectations for growth and adapt accordingly.

Provide the necessary infrastructure to support lifelong learning, such as learning management systems, access to educational resources, and opportunities for skill enhancement. Encourage collaboration and knowledge sharing among team members, as this fosters a culture of collective growth.

Lead by Example

The most powerful way to foster skill development and growth within your team is to lead by example. Just as the caterpillar's transformation serves as a natural model for its peers, your commitment to your own growth and development sets the standard for your team members.

Continuously seek opportunities to enhance your own skills and knowledge. Attend relevant training, engage in mentorship, and embrace challenges that push you out of your comfort zone. When your team sees your dedication to growth, they are more likely to follow suit.

By setting the example and creating a culture of growth, you contribute to the development of not only individual team members but also the organization as a whole. Your leadership legacy will be one of fostering lifelong learning, skill development, and a commitment to excellence.

Rise and Shine: Growth in Full Swing

In this chapter, we've embarked on a journey of growth and development, where your leadership serves as the nurturing force that encourages the potential within your team to flourish. Just as a gardener carefully tends to their plants, you cultivate an environment where growth is not just encouraged but celebrated, and where it is recognized as a continuous journey rather than a one-time event.

Picture your team as a vibrant garden, with each team member representing a unique plant that requires specific care and attention. Your role is that of a gardener and conductor, ensuring that every member receives the right amount of support and guidance to thrive. You provide the essential elements for growth, such as the sunlight of encouragement, the water of opportunities, and the soil of support.

But it's crucial to understand that growth is not a static destination; it's an ongoing journey. We've explored strategies to create a culture where feedback is cherished as a valuable gift, where failures are seen as stepping stones on the path to success, and where successes are celebrated as milestones of progress. By nurturing such a culture of growth, you're not only fostering individual advancement but also cultivating a collective mindset that propels your team toward limitless possibilities.

The Continuous Evolution

As a leader, your commitment to growth and development is not confined to the present moment. It's a continuous evolution, a journey that extends beyond the immediate horizon. Just as a garden changes with the seasons, your team is constantly evolving, learning, and adapting to new challenges and opportunities.

This journey requires a proactive approach to leadership. You actively seek out opportunities for your team members to grow, whether it's through delegation, shared decision-making, or skill enhancement. Like a gardener who prunes and nurtures their plants to encourage healthy growth, you trim away barriers and provide the nourishment your team needs to thrive.

Feedback: The Fertilizer of Growth

One of the essential elements for growth is feedback. Feedback serves as the fertilizer that enriches the soil of learning and development. It's the means through which your team members gain insights into their strengths and areas for improvement.

Effective feedback involves open communication, active listening, and constructive guidance. It's not about criticism but rather about providing insights and suggestions that help team members refine their skills and reach their full potential. Just as a gardener carefully observes the state of their plants, you attentively assess the progress of your team members and provide the necessary feedback to encourage their growth.

Failure as a Stepping Stone

Failure is an integral part of the growth process. In the garden of development, it's like the occasional storm that tests the resilience of the plants. Just as a gardener doesn't abandon their garden after a storm but assesses the damage and takes steps to restore it, as a leader, you don't abandon your team members when they encounter setbacks.

Instead, you view failure as a stepping stone on the path to success. Just as a plant may lose some leaves during a storm but continues to grow and thrive, your team members learn from their failures and use them as opportunities for improvement. Your role is to provide support and encouragement during these challenging times, helping them bounce back stronger and more resilient.

Celebrating Success: Milestones of Progress

In the garden of development, success is like the vibrant blossoms that signal the health and vitality of the plants. It's important to celebrate success as a milestone of progress. Just as a gardener admires and appreciates the beauty of their garden in full bloom, you acknowledge and celebrate the achievements of your team members.

Celebration is a powerful motivator that encourages team members to continue their growth journey. It recognizes their dedication and hard work and reinforces the value of their contributions. By celebrating success, you create a culture where accomplishments are appreciated and where team members are inspired to set higher goals and reach new heights.

Cultivating a Culture of Growth

Ultimately, your role as a leader is to cultivate a culture of growth within your team. This culture extends beyond the individual and becomes ingrained in the team's values and practices. It's a culture where feedback is embraced, where failure is viewed as an opportunity, and where success is celebrated.

Creating such a culture involves leading by example. Just as a gardener demonstrates proper care and attention to their plants, you exemplify the commitment to growth and development. Your actions and behaviors set the tone for the team, encouraging them to adopt a growth mindset and pursue their own development.

As a leader, you provide the infrastructure and resources necessary for growth to flourish. Just as a garden needs the right soil, sunlight, and water, your team requires access to training, mentorship, and learning opportunities. You create an environment where team members feel safe to share their ideas, express their concerns, and take ownership of their growth.

Unleashing Growth Potential

Your role as a leader is not limited to delegation, shared decision-making, or skill enhancement; it encompasses the orchestration of growth and development within your team. You serve as the catalyst that unleashes the growth potential within each team member.

Just as a conductor guides an orchestra to produce harmonious music, you guide your team toward new horizons of possibility. Your leadership shapes the symphony of growth and success, where each interaction, each decision, and each moment of growth contributes to the masterpiece of leadership excellence you're crafting.

In this flourishing garden of development, your nurturing touch serves as the catalyst that transforms potential into excellence. As you continue to cultivate an environment where growth is nurtured, celebrated, and embraced as an ongoing endeavor, you contribute not only to the current development of your team but also to a legacy of lifelong learning that will resonate through their careers and contribute to the enduring success of the organization.

Chapter 4

Problem-Busting and Change High-fives

Greetings, intrepid leader, and commander of the ship through the turbulent waters of challenge and change! In this captivating chapter, we embark on a dynamic journey into the heart of problem-solving and the art of managing transformation. As you step into your role as captain once again, you will tap into your inner superhero to confront obstacles, adopt a Sherlock Holmes-inspired mindset to unravel even the most perplexing conundrums, navigate through the tempestuous currents of change, and orchestrate high-fives of improvement that resonate throughout your team. So, prepare to set sail on this thrilling voyage of problem-solving and change management as we navigate through the challenges and triumphs that lie ahead.

The Challenge Awaits

In the ever-evolving landscape of leadership and team management, challenges are like formidable sea monsters that appear unexpectedly on the horizon. Just as a seasoned captain must be prepared to face a storm at sea, as a leader, you must be ready to confront and tackle these challenges head-on.

It's crucial to recognize that challenges are not necessarily obstacles to be feared; they are opportunities for growth and development. Just as a captain becomes more skilled and experienced by navigating through storms, your leadership abilities are honed through your encounters with challenges. These challenges can range from team conflicts and missed deadlines to budget constraints and market competition. Each presents a unique opportunity for you to showcase your problem-solving prowess.

The Sherlock Holmes Mindset

In the world of problem-solving, a Sherlock Holmes-inspired mindset is a valuable asset. Just as the great detective meticulously examines evidence, draws logical conclusions, and uncovers hidden truths, you, as a leader, must approach challenges with a keen eye for detail and a commitment to finding solutions.

To adopt a Sherlock Holmes-inspired mindset, you must first embrace the role of a detective. This involves gathering information, asking pertinent questions, and analyzing the situation from multiple angles. Just as Holmes searches for clues at a crime scene, you must search for the root causes of the challenges you face.

Next, like Holmes, you should exercise deductive reasoning. This means connecting the dots and drawing logical conclusions based on the information at hand. Just as Holmes pieces together a puzzle to solve a mystery, you must piece together relevant data to arrive at a solution.

Finally, emulate Holmes' determination and persistence. The great detective never gave up on a case, no matter how complex it was. Similarly, as a leader, you should demonstrate unwavering determination in the face of challenges. Embrace the challenge, seek creative solutions, and remain persistent in your quest for resolution.

Navigating the Winds of Change

Change is an inevitable force that impacts every organization and team. Just as a ship must navigate changing winds and currents, so must your team adapt to shifts in the business environment. Your role as a leader is to steer your team through these changes and help them adapt to new circumstances.

The first step in managing change is to acknowledge its presence and impact. Just as a captain must assess the strength and direction of the wind, you must assess the nature and scope of the changes affecting your team. Is it a minor adjustment, or a significant transformation? Understanding the magnitude of change is essential for planning the appropriate course of action.

Once you've assessed the changes, it's time to communicate effectively. Just as a captain must convey navigation instructions to the crew, you must communicate the details of the change to your team. Provide clear information about what is changing, why it's changing, and how it will impact the team. Open and honest communication builds trust and reduces uncertainty.

Collaboration is another key element in navigating change. Just as a ship's crew must work together to adjust the sails in response to changing winds, your team must collaborate to adapt to the evolving circumstances. Encourage team members to share their ideas and concerns, and involve them in the decision-making process where appropriate. Collaborative efforts will lead to smoother transitions.

In the face of change, it's important to remain flexible and adaptable. Just as a ship may need to adjust its course to respond to new wind patterns, your team may need to alter its strategies and approaches. Be open to experimenting with new solutions and be willing to make adjustments as needed.

High-Fives of Improvement

As a leader who guides their team through challenges and change, it's essential to celebrate victories along the way. Just as a captain acknowledges the crew's successful navigation through a storm, you should recognize and celebrate the achievements and improvements your team makes.

High-fives of improvement are moments when you acknowledge the team's progress and successes. These celebrations serve as positive reinforcement and motivation for your team to continue their problem-solving and adaptability efforts.

High-fives of improvement can take many forms, from verbal praise and recognition to tangible rewards or team-building activities. The key is to make these celebrations meaningful and tailored to the achievements. Just as a captain might host a special dinner for the crew after a successful voyage, you can create a special event or recognition to commemorate your team's accomplishments.

In addition to recognizing individual and team successes, high-fives of improvement also reinforce a culture of continuous growth and development. They emphasize the value of overcoming challenges and adapting to change, which further encourages your team to embrace these opportunities for improvement.

Setting Sail for Success

As you navigate through the uncharted waters of leadership, remember that challenges and change are not adversaries but opportunities for growth and transformation. With a Sherlock Holmes-inspired mindset, you can approach problems systematically and find innovative solutions. When facing change, acknowledge its presence, communicate effectively, foster collaboration, and remain flexible in your strategies. And always celebrate the high-fives of improvement, recognizing the accomplishments of your team.

You are the captain of your team's ship, steering it through the seas of challenge and change. The way you navigate these waters influences not only the team's ability to overcome obstacles but also its resilience and adaptability. With each challenge confronted, conundrum unraveled, and change managed, your leadership prowess grows, and your team becomes more skilled and agile.

So, batten down the hatches, my fellow captain of change, and set sail with confidence on this thrilling voyage of problem-solving and change management. As you lead your team through the challenges and triumphs that lie ahead, remember that it is through these experiences that your leadership legacy is shaped, and your team's potential is unlocked.

Tackling Troubles Head-On

Consider yourself a leader with unwavering determination and courage, poised to confront challenges with a blend of skill and expertise. In the realm of leadership, challenges are not insurmountable obstacles but opportunities for growth and innovation. Your strength lies in your ability to transform problems into stepping stones for success.

Problem-Solving Expertise

Your leadership approach to challenges mirrors that of a skilled problem-solver. Just as a detective delves into complex cases to unearth their mysteries, you dissect challenges to uncover their root causes. This involves a systematic approach to problem-solving, where you identify the core issues that require attention.

However, you don't navigate these challenges in isolation. You value collaboration and input from your team members. Effective problem-solving begins with clear communication and active listening. Encouraging your team to share their perspectives and insights is akin to a detective valuing witness statements.

Once you've gathered this information, the next step is to analyze it. This phase mirrors a detective's process of examining evidence. You identify patterns, connections, and potential causes of the challenge. This analysis leads to a deeper understanding of the issue at hand.

Creative Solutions

After a thorough understanding of the challenge is achieved, it's time to brainstorm and innovate. Just as a detective considers various scenarios to solve a case, you collaborate with your team to create inventive solutions. The key here is to think outside the box and explore unconventional approaches for effectively addressing the challenge.

Your superpower as a leader is your adaptability and resourcefulness. Just as superheroes face a variety of adversaries, you encounter diverse challenges in the realm of leadership. Being flexible and open to change enables you to respond effectively and find solutions that work.

Strength in Unity

The real magic of your leadership is in recognizing the strength in unity. Just as a superhero values teamwork, you involve your team in the problem-solving process, fostering a sense of shared ownership and responsibility. Challenges transform into rallying points under your leadership, motivating your team to face obstacles with newfound confidence and resilience.

Teamwork is paramount in your leadership, just as it is for superheroes like the Justice League or the Avengers. You harness the collective strengths and abilities of your team members, combining their skills for maximum impact.

You also foster a culture of shared ownership. Each team member becomes a stakeholder in addressing challenges and finding solutions. Your team takes on the responsibility of addressing challenges within the organization, much like superheroes protect the world.

Unleash Your Leadership Superpowers

To tackle challenges with the finesse of a seasoned leader, start by embracing your role with unwavering determination and courage. Just as superheroes hone their unique abilities, you must cultivate your leadership skills. This involves continuous development of your problem-solving prowess, decision-making abilities, and conflict resolution skills. Confidence in your leadership is your first superpower.

Your adaptability is another essential superpower. Just as superheroes face various adversaries, you will encounter a wide range of challenges in leadership. Being flexible and open to change allows you to respond effectively to different situations.

Effective communication and collaboration skills are also crucial superpowers. Just as superheroes work with allies to achieve their goals, you collaborate with your team to address challenges. Strong communication skills form the bridge that connects your superpower to the challenges at hand.

Empathy is an invaluable superpower in leadership. Understanding your team members' perspectives, concerns, and emotions is crucial. Empathy makes your leadership more relatable and impactful, allowing you to connect with your team on a personal level.

Problem-solving is at the core of your leadership superpower. Just as superheroes devise strategies to overcome adversaries, you develop strategies to tackle challenges. This involves critical thinking, analytical skills, and the ability to dissect complex issues. Problem-solving is where your superpower shines the brightest.

The Leadership Journey

In your leadership journey, you will confront numerous challenges, each an opportunity for growth and innovation. Just as superheroes inspire hope and courage, your leadership will motivate your team to face adversity with confidence and resilience. Embrace your role as a leader who can tackle challenges proactively, guiding your team toward success. With your leadership superpowers and your team's support, you can navigate through the challenges of leadership with unwavering determination and emerge victorious.

View Challenges as Opportunities:

Shift your perspective on challenges. Instead of seeing them as daunting obstacles, view them as opportunities for growth and innovation. This mindset shift can significantly impact how you and your team approach challenges. Encourage your team to embrace this perspective as well. Challenges become less intimidating when they're seen as stepping stones toward improvement.

The Art of Problem Dissection:

As an extraordinary leader, you possess the ability to dive deep into challenges. It's like being a detective uncovering clues. Invest time in understanding the root causes of issues. This involves asking probing questions, collecting data, and conducting thorough analyses. Your team should see you as someone who doesn't settle for surface-level solutions but seeks to understand the underlying problems.

Collaboration is Key:

Superheroes often have allies, and as a leader, your team is your greatest asset. Collaboration is not just about assigning tasks; it's about harnessing your team's collective intelligence. Encourage open dialogue, creative brainstorming, and open discussions to generate innovative solutions. Make sure team members feel comfortable sharing their insights and ideas.

Ownership and Responsibility:

Superheroes share their mission with allies, and you should share the problem-solving journey with your team. When team members are involved in the process, they develop a sense of shared ownership and responsibility. They're not just following your lead; they're active participants in finding solutions. This sense of ownership fosters unity.

Unity Through Challenges:

Your leadership can transform challenges into rallying points. Like a superhero leading their team into battle, your guidance should galvanize your team to face obstacles with newfound confidence and resilience. Team members should see you as a source of inspiration during tough times. Be transparent about the challenges you face and your strategy for overcoming them. This builds trust and respect.

Resilience and Learning:

Superheroes are known for their resilience, and as a leader, you must exhibit the same quality. Maintain composure under pressure, and communicate openly with your team during challenges. Emphasize the importance of learning from challenges, whether they end in success or failure. Conduct post-challenge debriefings to understand what worked, what didn't, and how you can improve.

Celebrating Together:

Lastly, don't forget to celebrate victories together. Publicly acknowledge and appreciate your team's efforts when a challenge is overcome. Share the story of how you collectively conquered adversity. Celebrations not only boost morale but also reinforce the idea that together, there's no obstacle too great. This strengthens the bond between you and your team.

By fully embracing your leadership superhero role, viewing challenges as opportunities, mastering the art of problem dissection, fostering collaboration, instilling a sense of ownership and responsibility, galvanizing unity, cultivating resilience, and celebrating victories, you'll not only tackle challenges head-on but also elevate your team's cohesion and respect for your leadership. You become the beacon of unwavering determination and courage that guides your team to success.

Solving with Smarts

In the realm of leadership, one of the most vital skills to master is problem-solving. As a leader, you often find yourself confronted with complex issues, and your ability to address them with precision and finesse can significantly impact your team's performance and cohesion.

Visualize each problem as a captivating puzzle, waiting to be solved through careful analysis and calculated reasoning. This perspective transforms problem-solving from a daunting task into an exciting challenge. When you approach problems with curiosity and enthusiasm, your team is more likely to adopt the same mindset.

Understanding the Core Issues:

When tackling problems, it's crucial to delve deep into complexity. Much like peeling the layers of an onion to reach its core, you must be willing to explore the intricacies of the issue at hand. Your role as a leader isn't limited to providing solutions; it also involves guiding your team on a journey of exploration and discovery.

Your team looks up to you for direction and insight. When they see you committed to understanding the core issues, it builds trust in your leadership. They know that you won't settle for surface-level solutions but will work tirelessly to uncover the root causes and develop effective strategies.

Nurturing a Culture of Curiosity:

Problem-solving isn't just about finding answers; it's about nurturing a culture of curiosity and critical thinking within your team. Encouraging your team to embrace the mindset of exploring problems as opportunities for growth and learning is essential.

Create an environment where team members feel comfortable asking questions, challenging assumptions, and experimenting with innovative solutions. When curiosity is encouraged and rewarded, it leads to more engaged and motivated team members.

Your Role as a Catalyst:

As a leader, you play a pivotal role in fostering a culture of curiosity. You can be the catalyst for intellectual pursuit within your team. Actively engage in discussions, seek diverse perspectives, and encourage open debates. Show your team that you value continuous learning and that you're always eager to explore new ideas and approaches.

When your team witnesses your dedication to intellectual growth, they are more likely to follow suit. They'll view problem-solving not as a solitary endeavor but as a collaborative effort where everyone's input is valued and appreciated.

Approaching Challenges with Enthusiasm:

The most successful leaders inspire their teams to approach challenges with enthusiasm. Instead of viewing obstacles as roadblocks, encourage your team to see them as opportunities for growth and development. Emphasize that each problem is a chance to exercise their mental faculties and contribute to the collective intelligence of the group.

Celebrate small victories along the way. When your team successfully overcomes a challenge, acknowledge their efforts and highlight the lessons learned. This reinforces the idea that challenges are not only manageable but also beneficial for personal and team growth.

Resilience in Problem-Solving:

Resilience is another key aspect of effective problem-solving. Just as a resilient individual can bounce back from setbacks, a resilient team can face challenges with determination and confidence. As a leader, it's essential to maintain composure under pressure and communicate openly with your team during challenging times.

Encourage your team to view setbacks as temporary and as opportunities to learn and improve. Develop a mindset of adaptability and flexibility, where adjustments and refinements are seen as natural parts of the problem-solving process.

Celebrating Successes:

Finally, don't forget to celebrate successes. When your team successfully tackles a problem or achieves a significant milestone, take the time to acknowledge their efforts. Share the story of how you collectively conquered adversity, highlighting the teamwork, creativity, and determination that led to success.

Celebrations not only boost team morale but also reinforce the idea that, together, there's no obstacle too great. This strengthens the bond between you and your team, fostering even greater respect and cohesion.

Mastering the art of problem-solving as a leader involves approaching challenges with curiosity and enthusiasm, understanding the core issues, nurturing a culture of curiosity, being a catalyst for intellectual pursuit, fostering resilience, and celebrating successes. By doing so, you not only excel as a leader but also inspire your team to respect your leadership even more, creating a cohesive and high-performing unit.

Navigating Change with Finesse

Change, often seen as a tumultuous force, can actually be harnessed as a powerful catalyst for growth and transformation. As a leader, your role in this process is akin to that of a skilled navigator, charting a course through the dynamic waters of change with finesse and determination. You aren't just a passive observer but an active guide, ensuring that your team not only survives the winds of change but thrives in their midst.

Leading Through the Evolving Landscape:

> Picture the landscape of change as a vast and ever-shifting terrain. Your role is not to shield your team from this transformation but to lead them through it. To do this effectively, ensure that everyone remains aligned, engaged, and enthusiastic about the journey ahead. Your leadership serves as the North Star, providing guidance and direction in uncertain times.

> Navigating change with finesse requires a deep understanding of its dynamics. Change is rarely a linear process; it can be tumultuous and disruptive. Your role is not to eliminate these challenges but to help your team navigate through them and here's how:

Effective Communication is Key:

> Change often brings uncertainty, and effective communication becomes paramount. You must not only convey the reasons behind the change but also the vision of what lies ahead. Transparency and openness are your allies. Keep the lines of communication open, and encourage your team to ask questions and express their

concerns. When they feel heard and informed, they are more likely to embrace change with enthusiasm.

Effective communication during times of change involves several key aspects:

Clarity: Ensure that your message is clear and easy to understand. Avoid jargon and technical language. Use simple and relatable examples to illustrate your points.

Consistency: Provide consistent messaging across all channels. Ensure that everyone in your team receives the same information, reducing confusion and rumors.

Two-Way Communication: Encourage an open dialogue. Listen actively to your team's concerns and feedback. Address their questions and acknowledge their fears.

Feedback Mechanisms: Establish feedback mechanisms that allow team members to share their thoughts and concerns anonymously if needed. This can provide valuable insights into the emotional and practical impact of the change.

Empathy: Acknowledge the emotional aspect of change. Understand that some team members may feel anxious, resistant, or even excited. Empathize with their feelings, and offer support where necessary.

Regular Updates: Keep your team informed about the progress of the change. Celebrate milestones and share success stories. This can boost morale and maintain momentum.

Managing Resistance with Empathy:

Resistance to change is a common human reaction. As a leader, it's your responsibility to understand and address this resistance with empathy and kindness. Seek to identify the root causes of resistance. Is it fear of the unknown, a perceived loss of control, or concerns about how the change will impact individual roles or positions? By addressing these concerns with compassion, you can help your team navigate through their apprehensions.

Empathy in managing resistance involves:

Active Listening: Pay close attention to what your team members are saying. Sometimes, they may not express their concerns directly but through subtle cues. Listen actively to both words and emotions.

Feedback Loops: Create feedback mechanisms that allow team members to voice their concerns and fears. Ensure that these channels are safe and non-judgmental.

Supportive Leadership: Be available to provide emotional support. Acknowledge the challenges of change and offer assistance when needed. Show that you are in this together.

Individual Conversations: If possible, have one-on-one conversations with team members who are particularly resistant. Understand their perspectives and work together on solutions.

Empowerment: Involve team members in decision-making related to the change when appropriate. This can give them a sense of control and ownership.

Cultivating a Sense of Purpose:

Change is most easily embraced when there's a sense of purpose behind it. As a leader, your role is to articulate the "why" of the change. What will it achieve for the team and the organization? How will it contribute to the bigger picture? When your team understands the purpose behind the change, they are more likely to embrace it as a necessary step on the journey toward greater success.

Cultivating a sense of purpose during change involves:

Storytelling: Use storytelling to illustrate the purpose of the change. Share stories of other successful transformations or individuals who have thrived in similar circumstances.

Vision Casting: Paint a compelling picture of what the future will look like after the change. Highlight the benefits and opportunities it will bring.

Alignment: Ensure that the change aligns with the core values and mission of your team and organization. When it fits into a broader narrative, it becomes more meaningful.

Relevance: Help each team member understand how the change is relevant to their role and their personal growth. When they see a direct connection, they are more likely to engage.

Adjusting the Sails:

Much like a skilled sailor adjusts the sails to catch the wind, you'll guide your team through each shift in the landscape of change. This involves being adaptable and flexible, ready to make course corrections as needed. Emphasize the importance of agility within your team, encouraging them to pivot when necessary and make the most of emerging opportunities.

Adjusting the sails in times of change involves:

Agility: Foster a culture of agility where your team is comfortable with change and quick to adapt. This involves a mindset shift that views change as an opportunity rather than a threat.

Learning Culture: Promote a learning culture within your team. Encourage continuous improvement and experimentation. When team members see change as a chance to learn and grow, they are more likely to embrace it.

Feedback-Driven: Use feedback loops to gather insights on the effectiveness of the change. If something isn't working as expected, be ready to make adjustments based on feedback.

Celebrating Wins: Recognize and celebrate small victories along the way. These milestones provide motivation and show that progress is being made.

Embracing Change as an Adventure:

Change is often viewed as a disruption, but your leadership can transform this perspective. Encourage your team to see change as an adventure, a thrilling journey into uncharted territory. Emphasize that, just as explorers discover new lands, your team has the chance to uncover new opportunities and avenues for growth through change.

Embracing change as an adventure involves:

Positive Framing: Frame change as a positive opportunity rather than a negative disruption. Highlight the exciting possibilities that lie ahead.

Risk-Taking: Encourage calculated risk-taking. Emphasize that stepping into the unknown can lead to remarkable discoveries and achievements.

Learning from Setbacks: Teach your team that setbacks are part of any adventure. Instead of seeing them as failures, view them as opportunities to learn and improve.

Shared Narrative: Create a shared narrative that paints the change as an epic journey. Use metaphors and stories to inspire a sense of adventure.

Instilling an Attitude of Open-Mindedness:

To make this mindset shift, foster an attitude of open-mindedness within your team. Encourage them to approach change with curiosity rather than apprehension. Highlight that every twist and turn in the journey brings new lessons and experiences. Your leadership should exemplify this attitude, showing your team that you are not just accepting of change but enthusiastic about the adventures it brings.

Instilling an attitude of open-mindedness involves:

Modeling Openness: Lead by example. Demonstrate your own open-mindedness and willingness to embrace change. Share stories of how change has personally enriched your life.

Encouraging Curiosity: Encourage your team to ask questions, explore new ideas, and seek innovative solutions. Create a safe space for them to express their thoughts.

Learning from Failure: Emphasize that failure is not a setback but a stepping stone to success. When your team members are open to experimentation, they are more likely to find innovative solutions.

Navigating change as a leader involves effective communication, empathy towards resistance, a sense of purpose, adaptability, and instilling an adventurous mindset. When you lead your team through change with finesse and enthusiasm, they are more likely to respect and trust your leadership, creating a cohesive and resilient unit ready to conquer new horizons.

By understanding the intricacies of navigating change, you can guide your team through even the stormiest of seas, emerging not only unscathed but stronger and more united than ever before. Your leadership, marked by effective communication, empathy and kindness, a clear sense of purpose, adaptability, and an adventurous spirit, becomes the beacon that lights the way through uncertainty and transformation. Embrace change as an opportunity for growth and encourage your team to embark on this exhilarating adventure with confidence and optimism.

Cultivating Camaraderie and Shared Achievement

Beyond the tangible aspects of improvement, it's essential to cultivate a spirit of camaraderie and shared achievement. Every small victory, regardless of its size, should be celebrated. Just as musicians in an orchestra share the joy of creating beautiful music, your team should share in the joy of achieving milestones. Here's how you can achieve this:

Acknowledging Contributions

Every contribution, no matter how minor it may seem, should be acknowledged and appreciated. When team members know that their efforts are noticed and valued, they feel motivated to continue their pursuit of excellence. Personalized acknowledgments, such as a simple thank you, go a long way in building morale.

Milestone Celebrations

Set milestones and celebrate them as a team. These celebrations can range from small gatherings or team lunches to more elaborate events. Milestones provide opportunities for reflection, recognition, and re-energizing the team for the journey ahead. They reinforce the idea that every step forward is a collective achievement.

Encouraging Peer Recognition

Create a culture where team members recognize and celebrate each other's contributions. Encourage peer-to-peer recognition programs or regular shout-outs in team meetings. When recognition comes from colleagues, it carries a unique sense of appreciation and fosters stronger bonds within the team.

Maintaining a Positive Atmosphere

Your leadership should maintain a positive atmosphere where victories are collectively savored and challenges are viewed as opportunities for growth. A positive atmosphere not only boosts morale but also makes your team more resilient in the face of difficulties.

Championing continuous improvement isn't just about processes and systems; it's about nurturing a culture of growth, innovation, and shared achievement. When your team sees you as a leader who not only advocates for improvement but actively participates in the journey, they will respect and admire your leadership even more. You'll be leading a team that's enthusiastic about innovation, resilient in the face of challenges, and eager to embark on a journey of perpetual refinement. Together, you'll create a harmonious symphony of progress that resonates throughout your organization.

So, my indomitable problem-buster, prodigious thinker of change, maestro of improvement, and conductor of celebration, prepare to elevate your leadership to new heights by embracing challenges, navigating change, and fostering improvement. As you journey through the realms of problem-busting and change high-fives, remember that each challenge conquered, each change navigated, and each improvement championed contributes to the symphony of leadership excellence you're composing.

Stay tuned as we approach the grand finale and unveil the captivating domain of team spirit spark!

Chapter 5

Team Spirit Spark

In this chapter, we will explore the dynamics of fostering a unified and enthusiastic team. We will delve into practical strategies to strengthen team unity and boost collective morale. You'll discover how to identify and nurture champions within your team, craft meaningful missions that inspire everyone, acknowledge and celebrate your team's efforts, and set a shining example as a leader. This chapter is all about practical guidance to enhance your team's spirit and performance. So, let's dive in and discover how to spark the spirit of teamwork and enthusiasm among your team members.

Spotlight on Success: Cheers for Champions

Imagine you are the orchestrator of a captivating light show, casting a brilliant spotlight on every achievement and triumph within your team. In this section, we will explore the art of celebrating success, infusing your team with renewed pride and motivation. Much like a spotlight draws attention to a central figure, your leadership will illuminate the extraordinary accomplishments of your team members, turning each victory into a radiant spectacle.

The Impact of Recognition

Recognition possesses the power to invigorate team members, providing the fuel for their souls to reach even greater heights. It's like a powerful motivator, inspiring individuals to push their boundaries and set new benchmarks. Your role as a leader is akin to that of a cheerleader, offering genuine praise and applause that resonates throughout your team, motivating them to continue their journey with a sense of purpose and fulfillment.

However, the true magic of recognition goes beyond celebrating success; it's about reinforcing the values and behaviors that contribute to that success. By shining the spotlight on accomplishments, you create a culture where dedication, innovation, and collaboration are consistently rewarded. Your leadership becomes the catalyst that transforms individual achievements into collective milestones, fostering a team that's motivated, engaged, and eager to conquer new horizons.

Strategies for Celebrating Success

Recognizing and celebrating success can take various forms, from simple affirmations to grand celebrations. The key is to choose the right approach based on the magnitude of the achievement and the preferences of your team members.

Individual Acknowledgment: A heartfelt one-on-one acknowledgment can go a long way. This personal touch conveys genuine appreciation for an individual's effort and dedication.

Team Celebrations: Recognizing the collective efforts of a team can create a sense of unity and camaraderie. Celebrations can be in the form of team lunches, outings, or group activities that promote bonding.

Public Acknowledgment: Sometimes, acknowledging success in a public forum, such as a team meeting or company-wide email, can boost team morale and inspire others.

Incentives and Rewards: Consider offering incentives or rewards for outstanding achievements. These can range from financial bonuses to extra time off or professional development opportunities.

Certificates and Trophies: Formal recognition in the form of certificates, trophies, or plaques can serve as lasting reminders of success.

Milestone Celebrations: Recognize key milestones and achievements, whether they are related to project completion, sales targets, or personal development goals.

Peer-to-Peer Recognition: Encourage team members to recognize and celebrate each other's successes. This peer acknowledgment fosters a positive and supportive team culture.

Creating a Culture of Recognition

To foster a culture of recognition within your team, consider the following strategies:

Consistency: Make recognition a regular part of your leadership. Celebrate both small and large successes to ensure that team members feel appreciated consistently.

Specific Feedback: When acknowledging success, be specific about what the individual or team did well. Specific feedback reinforces desired behaviors and accomplishments.

Alignment with Values: Ensure that recognition aligns with the core values and behaviors that are important to your team and organization.

Inclusivity: Celebrate successes across all levels and departments, creating a sense of equality and shared recognition.

Transparency: Be transparent about the criteria for recognition and ensure that it is applied consistently.

Feedback Loop: Encourage open communication by allowing team members to provide feedback on recognition processes and their preferences.

Impact on Team Motivation

The effects of recognizing and celebrating success extend beyond momentary morale boosts. They have a significant impact on team motivation and performance.

Increased Morale: Team members experience a boost in morale when their efforts are acknowledged. This positive reinforcement fosters a more enthusiastic and engaged team.

Enhanced Productivity: Motivated and engaged team members tend to be more productive. They are inspired to contribute their best to the team's success.

Greater Job Satisfaction: When team members feel recognized and appreciated, their job satisfaction increases, leading to higher retention rates and a more positive work environment.

Strengthened Team Cohesion: Celebrating successes together reinforces a sense of unity within the team. Team members become more cohesive and collaborative.

Empowerment: Recognition empowers team members to take ownership of their work and seek continuous improvement. It encourages a growth mindset and a desire to achieve further success.

The Role of Leadership

As a leader, you play a pivotal role in creating a culture of recognition and celebration. Here are some ways in which you can effectively lead in this regard:

Lead by Example: Be the first to recognize and celebrate success within your team. Your actions set the tone for the entire group.

Customize Recognition: Get to know your team members individually and understand how they prefer to be recognized. Tailor your approach to suit their preferences.

Stay Informed: Stay informed about team members' achievements and accomplishments. Don't rely solely on formal reports; actively seek out success stories.

Offer Constructive Feedback: In addition to celebrating success, offer constructive feedback that helps team members continue to grow and improve.

Promote Peer Recognition: Encourage team members to recognize and celebrate each other's successes. Create a culture where everyone participates in acknowledgment.

Celebrate Diversity: Recognize that each team member is unique, and their contributions are equally valuable. Celebrate diversity and the various strengths each individual brings to the team.

Building a legacy of recognition and celebration within your team can lead to enhanced motivation, increased productivity, and a more positive work environment. It's a leadership superpower that elevates team morale, fosters unity, and inspires your team to reach new heights of success. So, embrace your role as the orchestrator of success, and let your leadership shine the spotlight on your team's accomplishments, turning each achievement into a radiant spectacle.

Acknowledging the Power of Appreciation

In the realm of effective leadership, there exists a fundamental practice that is both potent and transformational: the sincere expression of appreciation and gratitude. Within this segment, we embark on a journey to explore the profound impact that stems from acknowledging the tireless efforts and invaluable contributions of your team members. The essence of this practice lies in the creation of an environment where the culture of appreciation is not a mere coincidence but a deliberate, integral part of your team's daily operations.

The importance of cultivating a culture of appreciation cannot be overstated. It goes beyond occasional recognition and extends to the very core of your team's dynamics. In this culture, appreciation is not a sporadic event but an ongoing, fundamental aspect of your team's interaction. It becomes as natural as any other element in your team's daily routines, and its presence is felt in every corner of your shared endeavors.

The impact of this appreciation is far-reaching. When team members feel genuinely valued and recognized for their efforts, their motivation soars. It ignites a spark within them, propelling them to reach for greater heights. They are not just cogs in a machine but individuals whose contributions are essential to the team's success.

This culture of appreciation serves as a powerful tool for building trust and rapport within your team. When team members know that their hard work will be acknowledged, it fosters an environment of openness and camaraderie. Communication becomes more transparent, and collaboration becomes second nature. Trust is the glue that binds a team together, and a culture of appreciation is a potent catalyst for its development.

But creating and sustaining this culture requires intention and commitment. It's not a mere checklist item but a mindset that leaders must adopt. It starts with being present and observant, actively looking for opportunities to express appreciation. It means recognizing not only the grand achievements but also the everyday contributions that often go unnoticed. It's about acknowledging that each team member, regardless of their role, brings something valuable to the table.

In this culture, leadership plays a pivotal role. Leaders are not just decision-makers; they are role models for the team. Their behavior sets the tone for the entire organization. When leaders consistently express appreciation and gratitude, it sets a powerful example for others to follow. It's a ripple effect that extends to every team member, creating a chain reaction of positivity and acknowledgment.

Appreciation also fuels a sense of ownership and pride in one's work. When team members know that their efforts matter, they take ownership of their tasks. They become more engaged in their work and take pride in the quality of their contributions. A culture of appreciation, therefore, isn't just about recognizing past achievements but also setting the stage for future successes.

The culture of appreciation is a practice that transforms the landscape of effective leadership. It's a profound acknowledgment of the efforts and contributions of team members, creating an environment where appreciation is a deliberate and fundamental part of daily operations. This culture fuels motivation, trust, collaboration, and a sense of ownership. It sets the stage for a team that is not just successful but also fulfilled and driven to achieve even greater heights. As a leader, embracing this culture is an investment that yields remarkable returns, both in the short term and in the enduring legacy of your leadership journey.

The Significance of Appreciation

Appreciation, within the realm of effective leadership, is a vital element that goes beyond mere compliments or occasional thank-yous. At its core, appreciation is about recognizing the intrinsic worth of each team member and the immeasurable value they bring to the collective effort. It's the act of validating their contributions and expressing genuine gratitude for the unique strengths they offer.

The true significance of appreciation becomes evident when we examine the ripple effect it has on a team's dynamics. It goes beyond simple recognition; it fosters a profound sense of belonging. In a culture of appreciation, individuals feel seen, heard, and valued for their distinct roles and contributions. It's the realization that they are not just a part of a team but an essential piece of the puzzle, vital to the team's success.

This sense of recognition is a powerful motivator. When team members know that their efforts matter and are genuinely appreciated, they are more likely to remain engaged, committed, and highly motivated. It ignites a spark within them, fueling their enthusiasm to go the extra mile and invest in the team's objectives.

Appreciation creates an atmosphere of trust and positivity within the team. When individuals feel valued and acknowledged, it cultivates trust and camaraderie. In such an environment, communication becomes more transparent and open. The barriers that often hinder effective collaboration start to crumble, and team members become more willing to share their ideas, feedback, and concerns.

Appreciation reinforces a sense of ownership and pride in one's work. Team members take their responsibilities more seriously when they know their contributions are not just recognized but celebrated. It's about fostering a sense of ownership in their tasks, instilling a belief that their role is vital in achieving the team's objectives.

In this culture of appreciation, leadership plays a pivotal role. Leaders set the tone for the entire organization. Their behavior, attitudes, and actions have a profound influence on the team. When leaders consistently express appreciation and gratitude, it creates a chain reaction of positivity that extends to every team member.

Leaders become role models, demonstrating the importance of recognizing the efforts and contributions of others. This consistent and sincere expression of appreciation sets a powerful example for others to follow, resulting in a team where appreciation is deeply embedded in its culture.

The impact of appreciation transcends the immediate and the individual. It extends to the team's collective achievements and long-term success. Team members who feel genuinely appreciated are more likely to be loyal to the organization, reducing turnover rates. They become more committed and motivated, resulting in enhanced productivity and better outcomes.

Appreciation is also a catalyst for personal and professional growth. When team members feel valued, they are more likely to invest in their development. They become open to feedback and learning opportunities, as they trust that their growth is encouraged and supported.

Appreciation is a cornerstone of effective leadership, serving as a fundamental and transformative practice. It creates a ripple effect that touches every aspect of a team's dynamics, from motivation and engagement to trust and collaboration. It fosters a culture of recognition, belonging, and pride in one's work. As leaders, embracing and nurturing this culture of appreciation is an investment with profound and enduring returns, both for the individual team members and the overall success of the team and organization.

The Role of a Leader in Cultivating Appreciation

In your role as a leader, you play a pivotal role in shaping your team's culture. Your actions, attitudes, and behaviors towards appreciation have a profound impact on the overall dynamics of your team. Think of yourself as the catalyst responsible for infusing positivity and warmth into the team's environment.

Leading by example is of paramount importance. As a leader, it is your duty to consistently and sincerely demonstrate appreciation. Your actions should serve as a model for your team members to follow. Express your gratitude openly during team meetings and in one-on-one interactions. Ensure that the recognition is not limited to significant accomplishments alone, but extends to the everyday efforts that contribute to the team's progress. This approach reinforces the fundamental belief that every team member's work holds meaning and significance.

When team members observe your appreciation and gratitude, they are more likely to adopt similar behaviors. Your actions serve as an inspiration, encouraging your team to express their appreciation towards each other and recognize the efforts of their peers. This ripple effect transforms your team into a cohesive unit, bound by mutual respect and gratitude.

In addition to your personal demonstration of appreciation, establish a system that institutionalizes the practice within the team. Implement regular recognition programs and channels that allow team members to acknowledge and appreciate each other. This creates a structured approach to appreciation, ensuring that recognition is a consistent and integral part of your team's culture.

Encourage your team to develop a habit of recognizing and appreciating one another. Highlight the importance of celebrating small wins, as well as significant achievements. This fosters an environment where team members genuinely value each other's contributions and understand the significance of collective effort.

As a leader, it is essential to provide timely and constructive feedback. Acknowledge areas of improvement and growth in addition to successes. Constructive feedback is a form of appreciation in itself, as it reflects your commitment to the professional development of your team members. By focusing on their growth, you demonstrate that you genuinely care about their progress and well-being.

To ensure that your team's culture of appreciation remains robust and continues to evolve, periodically revisit and assess the recognition programs and practices in place. Seek feedback from your team members to understand what forms of appreciation are most effective and meaningful to them. By involving your team in this process, you demonstrate your commitment to their well-being and your receptiveness to their needs.

As you establish and nurture a culture of appreciation, make it a point to create a sense of belonging within your team. Emphasize the idea that each team member is an indispensable part of the collective effort, and their unique contributions are essential to the team's success. When team members truly believe in their intrinsic value and significance, they are more likely to appreciate and recognize each other's efforts.

As a leader, your role in fostering a culture of appreciation is paramount. Your actions and attitudes towards appreciation serve as the catalyst that influences your team's dynamics. By leading by example, institutionalizing appreciation within your team, and encouraging a culture of mutual recognition, you can create an environment where team members genuinely value and appreciate each other. This sense of appreciation goes beyond words; it becomes a defining aspect of your team's identity, contributing to its cohesiveness, motivation, and overall success.

Methods of Expression

Appreciation can be expressed in various ways, both big and small. It's not limited to grand gestures or formal ceremonies; sometimes, the most genuine expressions of gratitude are simple and personal. Some methods to consider include:

Verbal Recognition: Publicly acknowledge achievements and contributions during team meetings. Highlight specific actions and their impact.

Personal Notes: A handwritten thank-you note or a heartfelt email can go a long way in expressing your gratitude. Personalize your messages to make them more meaningful.

Informal Conversations: Don't underestimate the power of casual conversations. Drop by a team member's workspace and express your appreciation for their dedication or a job well done.

Tokens of Appreciation: Small tokens or gifts, such as a gift card or a favorite snack, can convey your gratitude effectively.

Celebrations: Mark significant milestones and achievements for individual team members with celebrations. Whether it's lunch, a cupcake at their desk, or a virtual toast, these moments of joy reinforce a culture of appreciation.

Public Recognition: Highlight exceptional efforts on platforms accessible to the wider organization, such as newsletters, internal social media, or bulletin boards. Public recognition amplifies the positive impact.

Consistency Matters

One-off expressions of gratitude, while certainly valuable, may not be sufficient to create lasting change in your team's culture. To truly foster an environment where appreciation thrives, consistency is the key. As a leader, it's vital to make appreciation a regular and integral part of your leadership style. By integrating appreciation into your team's daily operations, you can ensure that it becomes a natural and expected aspect of their experience.

When appreciation becomes a consistent practice, it sends a powerful message to your team. It communicates that recognition and gratitude are not isolated events but an ongoing part of their work environment. This consistency reaffirms the importance of appreciation and its role in shaping the team's culture.

To achieve this consistency, consider incorporating appreciation into various aspects of your team's daily routine. For example, during team meetings, allocate time to acknowledge and celebrate achievements, both big and small. Encourage team members to express their gratitude towards one another openly.

Establish a system for providing feedback that includes expressions of appreciation. When you discuss performance and areas for improvement, remember to highlight the positive aspects and contributions of your team members. Let them know that their work is valued and recognized.

Another effective strategy is to have a dedicated platform or channel where team members can publicly acknowledge and appreciate each other's efforts. This can be an internal communication tool or a physical bulletin board in your workspace. Such platforms allow team members to express their gratitude in a visible and tangible manner, fostering a culture of appreciation.

Set an example by consistently practicing appreciation in your leadership role. Take the time to recognize and commend your team members for their contributions. Make it a habit to provide constructive and timely feedback that includes expressions of gratitude.

Consistency in appreciation also involves reinforcing the connection between achievements and recognition. When team members observe that their efforts lead to appreciation and acknowledgment, it motivates them to maintain high levels of performance. This recognition creates a positive feedback loop where the team members are driven to achieve more and better.

Consistency does not mean that appreciation should be routine or mundane. On the contrary, it should remain heartfelt and genuine. Team members can discern when appreciation is merely a formality, so it's crucial to ensure that it always carries sincerity and authenticity.

Consistency is the cornerstone of developing a culture of appreciation. It's about making gratitude an embedded and enduring part of your team's daily interactions. By doing so, you are actively contributing to a work environment where your team members feel valued, motivated, and eager to contribute their best efforts. This consistent practice of appreciation will shape your team's culture and inspire lasting change that goes beyond fleeting expressions of thanks.

Fostering Cohesion and Motivation

Beyond immediate morale-boosting effects, appreciation is a cornerstone of team cohesion. It reinforces a sense of unity and camaraderie. When team members feel appreciated, they are more likely to collaborate effectively, offer support to one another, and resolve conflicts constructively.

Appreciation also fuels motivation. It provides a sense of purpose and reinforces the idea that individual efforts contribute to the team's overall success. As a leader, this means your team is more likely to be motivated, engaged, and committed to achieving their shared goals.

Investing in the Future

Appreciation isn't just about the present moment; it's an investment in the future. By consistently expressing gratitude and cultivating a culture of appreciation, you're sowing the seeds for a team that's not only high-performing but also tightly knit, resilient, and committed to achieving greatness together.

Appreciation is a leadership practice that transcends the superficial and touches the core of effective team dynamics. It's about recognizing the intrinsic worth of each team member and expressing gratitude sincerely and consistently. When done right, it fosters a sense of belonging, unity, and motivation that propels your team toward achieving their shared goals. So, as a leader, consider appreciation as a powerful tool in your arsenal to create a positive and productive team environment.

Shine Bright: Your Awesome Example

Imagine your leadership as a radiant lighthouse, casting a reassuring glow that guides your team through the sometimes tumultuous waters of the professional world. Leading by example means embodying the very values and qualities you wish to see reflected in your team's actions. It's not just about talking the talk; it's about walking the walk.

Your consistency in your words and deeds is a source of inspiration for your team. It shows them the way forward with unwavering authenticity. It demonstrates that the principles you uphold aren't mere slogans but are deeply ingrained in your leadership style and are non-negotiable components of your professional character.

Leading by example also carries the weight of integrity. It's about doing what's right even when no one is watching. When your team witnesses your unwavering commitment to ethical conduct, it fosters a culture of trust and respect. Your integrity becomes a guiding principle, setting the tone for ethical behavior throughout your team.

When you consistently display integrity and live by the principles you preach, your team learns that ethical behavior isn't just a set of rules to be followed but a fundamental aspect of good leadership. They realize that integrity isn't a compromise, and that doing the right thing is not negotiable, regardless of the circumstances. Your example becomes a powerful force in shaping the ethical culture of your team.

The Transformative Power of Learning and Development

Your role as an exemplary leader goes beyond demonstrating excellence in your current skillset. It encompasses an active pursuit of self-improvement and a relentless thirst for learning. By embracing opportunities for growth, you not only elevate your own capabilities but also inspire your team with the transformative power of continuous development.

Your commitment to personal growth isn't just lip service; it's a living testament to the belief that learning is a lifelong journey. This commitment sets the stage for your team members to embark on their own journeys of growth and self-improvement. They see that leadership isn't about reaching a destination but about continuously striving for excellence.

Your pursuit of knowledge and skill development serves as a practical example of how to navigate the ever-changing landscape of the professional world. You demonstrate the value of adaptability and the importance of staying current in a rapidly evolving environment.

As you actively seek out new knowledge, skills, and experiences, you send a clear message to your team: stagnation is the antithesis of progress. You demonstrate that the pursuit of greatness requires stepping out of one's comfort zone, embracing challenges, and embracing the often uncomfortable but rewarding path of growth.

Cultivating Future Leaders

Your leadership isn't solely about achieving your team's immediate objectives; it's also about nurturing the leaders of tomorrow. When you lead by example, you empower your team members to become leaders in their own right. Your actions provide them with a blueprint for effective leadership that they can carry forward in their careers.

As you consistently embody the qualities of an exemplary leader—integrity, humility, dedication, and a commitment to growth—you set a standard that your team members aspire to achieve. They understand that the path to leadership is not exclusive; it's inclusive and accessible to anyone who's willing to embrace it.

Your example becomes a touchstone for excellence, encouraging your team members to push their limits, embrace challenges, and strive for greatness. It instills a sense of responsibility and ownership in them, as they see the impact that individual actions can have on the team's overall success.

Your mentorship goes beyond formal training programs or leadership development initiatives. It's a day-to-day, real-life demonstration of effective leadership. Your team members can observe and learn from your actions, decisions, and interactions, gaining insights into how to navigate complex situations, inspire others, and foster a positive team dynamic.

The Ripple Effect of Positive Change

Leading by example has a ripple effect that extends far beyond the boundaries of your immediate team. It influences the wider organization's culture and the way leadership is perceived and practiced. Your commitment to professionalism, dedication, and integrity becomes a source of inspiration and admiration for others.

Your leadership style sets a standard for excellence that others may seek to emulate. This, in turn, elevates the overall quality of leadership within the organization. It fosters an environment where ethical behavior, continuous growth, and authentic leadership are not just ideals but lived realities.

When other leaders and team members witness the positive impact of your leadership style, they are encouraged to adopt similar approaches. This cultural shift can lead to a more cohesive and harmonious work environment, where teams are guided by strong ethical principles, motivated by continuous improvement, and inspired by the authentic leadership they observe.

Leading by example is a powerful and multifaceted aspect of leadership. It involves embodying the values and qualities you wish to see in your team's actions, demonstrating unwavering integrity, and actively pursuing personal growth. It's about inspiring and empowering your team members to become leaders in their own right and fostering a culture of excellence and authenticity. As you shine brightly in your role as an exemplary leader, you not only guide your team towards success but also contribute to a positive transformation in the wider organizational landscape. Your example becomes a lasting legacy, inspiring others to follow in your footsteps and continue the tradition of exemplary leadership.

In Summation

As you traverse the realms of celebrating success, crafting meaningful missions, expressing gratitude, and leading by example, you're orchestrating a symphony of unity and positivity that reverberates throughout your team. Each action you take, each gesture you make, and each moment you create contributes to the vibrant tapestry of team spirit that you're cultivating.

Remember, your leadership isn't just about achieving goals; it's about nurturing a sense of purpose, fostering a deep sense of belonging, and inspiring your team to achieve their best. As you continue on your journey, leading with an open heart and a genuine desire to uplift those around you, you'll witness the transformative power of team spirit spark in action.

So, my extraordinary conductor of camaraderie, let your leadership shine as a guiding star, inspiring your team to reach for the heavens and embrace the boundless possibilities that await them. Your role as a champion of team spirit is nothing short of magical, and your influence will leave an indelible mark on the hearts and minds of all who have the privilege of being led by you.

Bravo, and may your symphony of leadership continue to resonate in the hearts of your team members for years to come!

Conclusion

As we reach the end of our journey, it's time to pause, reflect, and celebrate the remarkable adventure you've undertaken. Throughout this book, you've embarked on a voyage of self-discovery, honed your leadership skills, and delved into the realms of connection, collaboration, problem-solving, and team spirit.

As you stand at the precipice of this conclusion, let's raise a virtual toast to the magnificent odyssey you've embraced. Cheers to your unwavering dedication to becoming the best leader you can be, and here's to the incredible impact you'll make on your team, organization, and beyond.

Ready, Set, Go: Supercharge Your Skills

Reflect on your journey through the pages of this book, and imagine yourself at the starting line of a thrilling race – a race to supercharge your leadership skills and blaze a trail of excellence. Just as a seasoned athlete fine-tunes their body and mind, you've equipped yourself with a toolkit of practical and impactful leadership principles.

Think of each chapter as a training ground, where you've honed your abilities to connect authentically, collaborate synergistically, navigate challenges confidently, and ignite team spirit passionately. Your readiness is a testament to your commitment to growth and your enthusiasm to embrace the full potential of your leadership.

Picture yourself poised for action, eager to implement the lessons you've learned and lead with renewed purpose. Armed with the insights and strategies from this book, you're prepared to step onto the track of leadership with a newfound energy and confidence. Your journey is just beginning, and the road ahead is paved with opportunities to apply your enhanced leadership skills in real-world scenarios.

Planting Seeds for a Future of Fantastic Leadership

Just as a gardener plants seeds with care and cultivates them with dedication, you've sown the seeds of fantastic leadership that have the potential to flourish and bear fruit for years to come.

Consider each principle, each idea, and each strategy you've encountered as a seed planted in the fertile soil of your leadership foundation. With each application and practice, you're providing the essential nutrients of dedication, perseverance, and continuous learning. These seeds of wisdom and insight will sprout into a lush landscape of exceptional leadership, shaping your future and the future of those you lead.

Envision a future where your leadership is characterized by authentic connections, collaborative brilliance, adept problem-solving, and a vibrant team spirit. As you water and nurture these seeds of growth, your influence will spread far and wide, touching the lives of your team members, peers, and anyone fortunate enough to cross paths with your leadership journey.

Finally...

And so, dear leader, we come to the end of this remarkable adventure – an adventure that's only the beginning of your journey toward becoming an exceptional leader. As you reflect on the pages turned and the lessons learned, remember that leadership is not a destination; it's a continuous journey of growth, discovery, and impact.

As you close this book, carry with you the wisdom you've gained and the friendships you've forged with the ideas and principles presented. Embrace the challenges that come your way as opportunities for growth and approach each day as a chance to embody the leadership excellence you've cultivated.

Your leadership adventure is unique, filled with twists, turns, and breathtaking moments of inspiration. Embrace it with open arms, knowing that you have the power to create a legacy of positive change, a legacy that will ripple through time and touch the lives of those you lead.

So, my fearless trailblazer of leadership, go forth and lead with heart, with purpose, and with the unwavering belief that you have the capacity to make a profound difference. Your journey has only just begun, and the path ahead is illuminated by the radiant glow of your potential. May your leadership story be one of growth, connection, and the pursuit of greatness.

Congratulations on completing this incredible leadership adventure – and now, my friend, it's time for you to lead the way!

Leadership Playbook

As you wrap up this enriching journey through the art of practical leadership, it's time to equip yourself with some bonus tools and resources to keep the leadership fire burning bright. Welcome to the Leadership Playbook, your go-to guide for further exploration, self-assessment, and a treasure trove of online goodies that will elevate your leadership game. So, without further ado, let's dive into this friendly and resourceful appendix!

Top Reads to Keep the Leadership Fire Burning

Imagine yourself in a cozy reading nook, surrounded by a stack of books that promise to fuel your leadership journey with inspiration and insight. Here are twenty must-read leadership books that will keep your leadership fire burning long after you've closed the pages of this book:

1. "Dare to Lead" by Brené Brown
2. "Leaders Eat Last" by Simon Sinek
3. "The 5 Levels of Leadership" by John C. Maxwell
4. "Good to Great" by Jim Collins
5. "Drive: The Surprising Truth About What Motivates Us" by Daniel H. Pink
6. "Start with Why" by Simon Sinek
7. "Mindset: The New Psychology of Success" by Carol S. Dweck
8. "Radical Candor" by Kim Scott
9. "Emotional Intelligence" by Daniel Goleman
10. "The Lean Startup" by Eric Ries
11. "The Power of Habit" by Charles Duhigg
12. "Multipliers: How the Best Leaders Make Everyone Smarter" by Liz Wiseman
13. "Crucial Conversations" by Kerry Patterson, Joseph Grenny, Ron McMillan, and Al Switzler

14. "Leadership and Self-Deception" by The Arbinger Institute

15. "The One Minute Manager" by Ken Blanchard and Spencer Johnson

16. "Leadership Is an Art" by Max DePree

17. "The Innovator's Dilemma" by Clayton M. Christensen

18. "The Art of Possibility" by Rosamund Stone Zander and Benjamin Zander

19. "Grit: The Power of Passion and Perseverance" by Angela Duckworth

20. "Atomic Habits" by James Clear

These books offer a variety of perspectives, insights, and practical strategies to enhance your leadership skills and mindset. Each title is a valuable addition to your leadership library, providing you with the knowledge and tools to continue your journey of growth.

Super Self-Check: How's Your Leadership Mojo?

Picture yourself in front of a funhouse mirror, reflecting on your leadership journey with a curious and introspective gaze. In this section, we've crafted a super self-check that allows you to assess your leadership mojo in a lighthearted and engaging way. Think of it as a playful quiz designed to help you gauge your progress, identify areas of strength, and uncover opportunities for further development.

1. Are you actively seeking feedback from your team members and peers?

2. Do you consistently set clear goals and expectations for your team?

3. How do you handle challenging situations or conflicts within your team?

4. Are you open to trying new approaches and experimenting with innovative ideas?

5. How do you cultivate a culture of trust and psychological safety within your team?

6. Are you effectively communicating your vision and goals to your team?

7. How do you empower your team members to take ownership of their work and projects?

8. Are you actively fostering an environment of diversity and inclusion within your team?

9. How do you prioritize self-care and well-being as a leader?

10. How do you celebrate and acknowledge the achievements and contributions of your team members?

This self-check isn't about judgment or evaluation; it's about self-awareness and growth. It's an opportunity to celebrate your victories, acknowledge your growth, and set intentions for your future as a leader. As you respond to the thought-provoking questions, remember that every step of your leadership journey is a valuable experience, whether it's a triumphant moment or a lesson learned.

By engaging in this self-check, you're giving yourself the gift of reflection – a chance to pause, assess, and realign your leadership compass. Embrace it with an open heart and a willingness to embrace both your strengths and areas for improvement. Your leadership mojo is a dynamic force that evolves with every step you take, and this self-check is a delightful way to keep your leadership journey on track.

Extra Boost: Online Goodies for Leadership Enthusiasts

Here is a useful digital treasure chest of leadership goodies that will supercharge your growth and keep your enthusiasm for leadership burning bright! In this section, we've curated a selection of online resources, courses, podcasts, and communities that are tailored for passionate leadership enthusiasts like you. Whether you're seeking to expand your skill set, engage in thought-provoking discussions, or connect with fellow leaders, these online gems have got you covered.

Here are twenty online resources to explore:

1. **Coursera** - Offers a wide range of leadership courses from top universities and institutions.

2. **edX** - Provides online courses on leadership, management, and related topics.

3. **LinkedIn Learning** - Features a plethora of leadership and professional development courses.

4. **Harvard Business Review** - Offers articles, videos, and online courses on leadership and management.

5. **Toastmasters International** - Provides resources and clubs for improving public speaking and communication skills.

6. **MindTools** - Offers a variety of leadership and management resources, including articles, quizzes, and worksheets.

7. **Leadership Freak Blog** - A blog by Dan Rockwell with insightful articles on leadership.

8. **TED Talks** - Features numerous inspiring talks on leadership and personal development.

9. **Fast Company** - Provides articles and insights on leadership, innovation, and business trends.

10. **The Center for Creative Leadership** - Offers research and resources on leadership development.

11. **Seth Godin's Blog** - A blog by Seth Godin with thought-provoking insights on leadership and marketing.

12. **Harvard Business Review Podcasts** - Podcasts that cover a wide range of leadership and business topics.

13. **The John Maxwell Company** - Offers leadership resources, books, and training programs.

14. **Michael Hyatt's Leadership Podcast** - Podcast episodes on leadership, productivity, and personal development.

15. **Simon Sinek's Start With Why** - Explore Simon Sinek's work on leadership and purpose.

16. **The Leadership Circle** - Provides tools and assessments for leadership development.

17. **IDEO U** - Offers design thinking and innovation courses that can enhance your leadership skills.

18. **Center for Humane Technology** - Explores the ethical and social implications of technology leadership.

19. **Management Study Guide** - Offers a variety of resources on management and leadership topics.

20. **Berkeley Executive Education** - Provides executive education programs on leadership and strategy.

Embrace the digital landscape as an extension of your leadership playground, and feel free to tailor your online exploration to your unique interests and aspirations.

Dear Reader,

As you close the final chapter of this book, please know that I greatly appreciate you taking this journey with me. It has been an honor to share my insights and experiences in the hope that they may empower you on your own leadership path.

My wish is that these pages have illuminated new perspectives, equipped you with practical skills, and ignited your passion for unlocking your leadership potential. May the lessons distilled here serve you well as you cultivate influence, inspire teams, and make a positive impact wherever you go.

Though our time together through these chapters is ending, remember that your leadership journey has just begun. Approach it with courage, compassion, and commitment to leaving people and places better than you found them.

You now hold many of the tools to become the remarkable leader you were meant to be. Believe in your abilities and lead from the heart. I am cheering you on!

With gratitude and confidence in your future success,

Jan Corder Heminger

Contact Information:
Jan@SpokenWordEngage.com
www.SpokenWordEngage.com
We welcome feedback and comments!
Visit our website for more lifechanging information!